THE CHEQUERS

DEDICATION.

TO
PHILIP WOOD AND JOHN WOOD,
OF
SOUTH SHIELDS.

GENTLEMEN,—This record of ruined lives is inscribed to you, for it is mainly owing to you that I have gained such gruesome experience. From the day when, as a boy of seventeen, I formed my connection with your honourable house, I have owed my professional success to your culture, your generosity, and your admirable relations with the police force. My Sovereign and many other people have been pleased to approve my strange labours; but my chief distinction in life arises from my being your relative. With feelings which I cannot describe,

I remain,
Your obliged and grateful,

JAMES RUNCIMAN.

CONTENTS

INTRODUCTION.

It is risky to go home with some of the company from the Chequers, for good-fellowship is by no means fostered in the atmosphere of a public-house. The creatures who write about the cheerful glass, and the jovial evening, and the drink that mellows the heart, know nothing of the sad work that goes on in a boozing-place, while the persons who draw wild pictures of impossible horrors are worse than the hired men who write in publican's papers. It is the plain truth that is wanted, and one year of life in a public-house teaches a man more than all the strained lectures and colourless statistics. I am going to give a series of pictures that will set forth every phase of public-house life. It is useless to step casually into a bar, and then turn out a flashy article. If you want to know how Drink really acts on the inner life of this nation you must actually live among the forlorn folk who drink Circe's draught, and you must live as their equal, their friend, their confidant. I am a Loafer, and not one of the gang at The Chequers would ever dream of regarding me as anything but an equal. My friend Donkey Perkins, the fighting man, curses me with perfect affability and I am on easy terms with about one hundred costermongers. If a "gentleman" went among them he could learn nothing. Observe the hush that falls on the babble of a tap-room if any well-dressed person goes in; listen to the hum of warning, and then notice the laboured hypocrisy of the talk that goes on so long as the stranger is there. I have seen that odd change scores of times, and I know that nothing can be more curious than the contrast between the scrappy, harmless chat that goes on while the representative of respectability is there, and the stupid, frank brutalities which the advent of the visitor silenced.

At nights I go home with one after another of my set, and at merry seasons we stay together till early morning. They throw off all disguise before me, and even the thieves are not afraid. When once you are on level terms with the community you begin to see what is the true result of drink. The clergyman, the district visitor, the professional slummer—all the people who "patronise"—never learn the truth, and they positively invite the wastrel classes to lie.

Some time ago I read some "revelations" which made a great stir in the country. The writer was accused of publishing obscenities, but what struck me most in his work was its absolute display of ignorance. The poor, innocent man had listened to stories which were told in the dialect that is used to impress outsiders, and I laughed as I seemed to hear the very tones of some shady gentry of my own acquaintance. The unhappy vendor of revelations went among his subjects of study for six weeks, and then set up as an authority. Of course, the acute, sleazy dogs whom he questioned kept back everything that was essential, and filled their victim's mind with concoctions which amused professional blackguards for a month. Could that literary adventurer only have heard the criticism which daily met my ear, he would have found that many eager souls were longing for a chance to plunder such an obvious "mug." Another writer, whose works appear in a morning journal, professes to make flying visits to various queer places, and his articles are published as facts; but I had the chance of testing the truth of two tales which dealt with official business, and I found that these two were false from end to end. Not only were they false, but they illustrate nothing, for the writer did not know the conditions of the life which he pretended to describe, and his fiction misled many thousands. Experience, then—sordid, miserable, long experience—is needed before anyone can speak the truth concerning the life of what Carlyle called "the scoundrel classes." The same experience only can teach you anything about the poor. The scoundrels do not actually confide in anybody, and I never yet knew one of them who would not turn on a confederate; but they exhibit themselves freely before people to whom they have become used. It unfortunately happens that the scoundrels and the dissolute poor are much thrown together. A man may be a hopeless drunkard without being a rascal, but the rascals and the boozers are generally taken in the lump by persons of a descriptive turn of mind. That is faulty natural history. The chances are always ten to one in favour of the boozer's becoming a criminal; but we must distinguish between those who have taken the last bad step and those who are merely qualifying. And now for our history.

THE WANDERER.

The bar was very much crowded last night, and the air was impregnated to choking point with smoke and evil exhalations. The noisy times on Saturdays come at 2 p.m., and from ten till closing time. In the afternoon a few labourers fuddle themselves before they go home to dinner, and there is a good deal of slavering incoherence to be heard. From seven to eight in the evening the men drop in, and a vague murmur begins; the murmur grows louder and more confused as time passes, and by ten o'clock our company are in full cry, and all the pipes are in full blast. When I stole quietly in, I thought the scene was hideous enough in its dull way. The gas flared with drowsy refulgence through the reek, and the low masks of the roaring crew somehow left on me an impression that I was gazing on *one* bestial, distorted face. A man who is a racecourse thief and "ramper" hailed me affably. A beast of prey he is, if ever there was one. His hatchet face with its piggish eyes, his thin, cruel lips, his square jaw, are all murderous, and, indeed, I cannot help thinking that he will commit a murder some day. When he is in his affable mood he is very loathsome, but I cannot afford to loathe anyone, and we smile and smile, though we dislike each other, and though the Ramper hardly knows what to make of me. When I first made his acquaintance we were on our way to a race meeting, and he proposed to give me his company. Like all of his class, he knew many "certainties," and he offered, with engaging frankness, to put me in the way of "gittin' a bit." The racing blackguard never talks of money; indeed, his obliquity of mind prevents him from calling anything by its right name. For him the world is divided between those who "have got it"—*it* being money—and those who mean to "get a

15

bit" by any means, fair or foul. On that day, long ago, this creature fancied that I had some money, and he was determined, to rob me somehow. I let him imagine that he was leading me on, for there is no luxury that I enjoy more than watching a low, cunning rogue when he thinks he is arranging a successful swindle. I was introduced to a thoroughly safe man. The safe man's face was almost as villanous as that of my mentor, and his manners were, perhaps, a little more offensive. Our first bet closed all transactions between us; as I fully expected, I obtained a ridiculously liberal price, and I *won*. On my proposing a settlement, the capitalist glared virtuously and yelled with passion—which was also what I expected. Then came my mentor, and softly remarked, "Don't go and queer his pitch. Here's a lot on 'em a-comin', and they'll be all over you if you say a word. Wait till he gits a bit and he'll pay." This was also what I expected. We happened to be in an enclosed ground, so I managed to keep my eye on the capitalist, and the unhappy being vainly strove to dodge away. Catching him in the act of sneaking through the turnstile, I touched him gently, and then beckoned to a policeman. No welsher can hope for admission to one of the enclosed courses after he is once fairly caught, and my victim whimpered, "Come in yere and 'ave a drink." Then he said, "Look yere, I ain't got a bloomin' 'alf dollar but what I 'ad off o' you. I walked down this mornin', and hadn't only the gate-money, and your pal laid me on to you. Say nothin' this time. I ain't had no grub today. Give us a chance. 'Twas your pal as put me on, mind. Brandy cold, if you don't mind."

The ineffable impudence of the capitalist's request made it hard for me to keep from laughing; I let him go, and I fear that he and the Ramper made further attempts on the idiots who throng the Silver Ring.

That same evening Mr. Ramper made his last effort to practise on me. We were straddling among a sporting group in The Chequers bar, when he said, "Better settle over Dexter." "Dexter? What about Dexter?" "Didn't you take Dexter agin' Folly?" "Not such a mug." Then the hound raised his voice in the fashion of his tribe. "You goin' to welsh me, are you? You don't mean to pay that ten bob? I'll 'ave it out of your bloomin' liver!" All this was uttered in a yell which was intended to draw attention, and the creak of the brute's voice made me inclined to dash my fist in his vile face. But I only grinned and said "What a poor liar you are."

The more the Ramper screeched, the more I laughed; he durst not strike, and at last, when I reminded him that he had already divided a little plunder with the capitalist, he grumbled a curse or two and lapsed into affability. You cannot shame one of these beings, and the Ramper is now on the most confidential terms with me. I am very glad we did not fight, because he introduced me to one of the most interesting and estimable of all my acquaintances. Said the Ramper, blowing his sickly breath into my very ear, "There's a bloke yere as knows suthin' good for Lincoln. Up in the corner there. Let's sit down." Within a minute I found myself talking to a queer, battered man, who bent moodily over his glass of gin and stole furtive glances at me with bleared, sullen eyes. His blood was charged with bile, and he could not prevent the sudden muscular twitchings of his hands. His knuckles were swollen, and his fingers were twisted slightly. Evidently he was diseased to the very bone through alcoholic excesses. He was dressed in a shiny overcoat, and his bony shanks threatened to pierce his trousers. When he pushed back his rakish greasy hat, he showed a remarkably fine forehead—well filled, strong, square—but he had the weakest and most sensual mouth I ever saw. There was scarcely a sign of a lower jaw, and the chin retreated sharply from the lip to the emaciated neck.

My man spoke with a deep voice that contrasted oddly with his air of debility, and I noticed that he not only had a good accent, but his words were uttered with a deliberate attempt at formal and polished elocution. We talked of horse-racing, and he mouthed out one speech after another with a balanced kind of see-saw, which again and again ran into blank verse. I said, "You have something good for Lincoln, I hear. Any chance of being on?" He replied, "I heed no fairy tales or boasting yarns. When a man says he has a certainty, I tell him to his face that he's a liar. The ways of chance are far beyond our ken, and I can but say that I try.

17

Information I have. From Newmarket I receive daily messages, and I have as much chance of being right as other men have; but you know what the Bard says. Ah! what a student of human nature that man was! What an intellect! In apprehension how like a god! You know what he says of prophecy and chance? I only fire a bolt at a venture, and if my venture don't come off, then I say, 'Pay up and look pleasant.'"

The majestic roll of his speech was very funny, and he poured forth his resonant periods as though I had been standing at a distance of twenty yards. As the gin stirred his sluggish blood he became more and more declamatory, and when at last he fairly yelled, "I am a gambler. I could not brook life if I had no excitement. It is my very blood. Yet, think not my words are false as dicers' oaths," and waved his right hand with a lordly gesture, I thought, "An old actor, for certain." So long as his senses remained he talked shrewdly about betting, and his remarks were free from the mingled superstition and rascality which make ordinary racing talk so odious; but when he began to drink rapidly he soon became violent, and finished by carrying on like a madman. He shouted passages from "Hamlet" and "Coriolanus" with ear-splitting fervour, and at last he drew a universal protest from the rest of our crew, who are certainly not sensitive. Then his yell grew maudlin. "Why did God make me thus? Why do I grunt and sweat under the burden of a weary life? Give me, ah, give me the days that are gone!" Then he fell alongside of the bench, and presently his long, gurgling snore sounded fitfully. "Let him sweat there till closing time; he'll be quiet enough," said Mr. Landlord; and sure enough the orator lay until the hour had struck. He shivered when he rose, and his knees were like to fail him. "Heavens! what a mouth I've got!" he moaned, and I could see that the deadly, bitter fur had already covered his palate. "Take a flask home, Billy, and pull yourself together when you turn in." Billy grabbed fiercely at the air. "These infernal flies have started early." The specks were dancing before his eyes, and I fancy he had an ugly night before him; but I didn't see him home.

THURSDAY.—I have found out a good deal about my stagy friend, and we are quite confidential, especially late at night. He weeps plenteously and recalls his own sins, but I think he is fairly truthful. A moving, sordid history is his. Moralising is waste of time, but one might almost moralise to the extent of boredom concerning the life of Billy Devine, boozer, actor, betting-man.

Devine's peculiarly grandiose mode of telling his story was rather effective at first hearing, but it would read like a burlesque, so I translate his narrative into my own dialect. He was a quick, clever lad, and the culture bestowed in a genteel academy was too narrow for him. He read a great deal of romance, and still more poetry. He neglected his school lessons, and he was dismissed after a few years as an incurable scamp.

No sort of steady work suited Devine; his fatal lack of will was supplemented by an eager vanity, and he was only happy when he was attracting notice. Now that he is matured, he is gratified if he can make drunken costermongers stare, so he must have been a very forward creature when his conceit was in full blossom. He began by spouting little recitations, and gradually practised until he could take his part in amateur stage performances. As he put it, "I found that the majesty of Coriolanus and the humour of Paul Pry were alike within my compass, and I impartially included both these celebrated parts in my *répertoire*." Nothing ever diverts a stage-struck youth from his fell purpose unless he is absolutely pelted off the boards. Devine loathed his office; he hated the sight of a business letter, and he finally appeared in a wretched provincial booth, where he earned seven shillings per week in good times: the restraints of respectability were to hamper him no more. Through all his miserable wanderings I tracked him, for he kept playbills, and each bill suggested some quaint or sordid memory. I felt something like a lump in my throat when he said, "Now, dear friend, at this place I played once the 'The Stranger' and 'The Idiot Witness,' and for two days my comrade and I had nothing to eat. On one eventful night we saw some refuse fish being wheeled off in a barrow, and we begged leave to abstract a fish, which was—I say it without fear of contradiction—the knobbiest and scaliest member of the finny tribe. Sir, we tried to skin this animal and failed. Then we scraped him, and the moving question arose, What about fire? Luckily the landlady had left a lamp on the stairs. My inventive faculties were bestirred. The LAMP! No sooner said than the fish was placed on the fire-shovel, and we then took turns to move the shovel backwards and forwards over the lamp. Regardless of that woman's loud inquiries about the smell, which was in truth, sir, very overpowering, we pursued our joint labours until two in the morning, and then the brute was only *half* raw. One penknife was our sole cutlery; but we managed to cut through the skin, and we devoured the oily stuff like famished hounds, sir. We were ashamed; but, as the poet truly observes, 'Necessity knows no law,' and we endured the scurrilous language of the woman when, on the morrow, she found the bottom of the shovel encrusted with dirt and the top thickly coated with grease. That fish saved us, sir."

Little by little Devine worked his way towards London, and at length he appeared in a West-end theatre. His reminiscences of the stars are impressive, but we need not deal with them; it is enough to say that he was successful—and in light comedy no less. About this time he began to have his photograph taken very frequently, and the portraits made me feel sad. This dull, sodden man was once a handsome fellow, alert, well poised, brave and cheerful. The profile which I saw in the photographs somehow made me think of an arrow-head on the upward flight; that, lower jaw, which is now so flabby and slobbery was once well rounded, and the weakness was not unpleasantly evident. I often wonder that human vanity has not done away with alcoholism. Men are vain animals, yet a good-looking fellow, who could never pass a mirror without stealing a quiet look, will cheerfully go on drugging himself until every feature is transformed. I have seen the process of facial degradation carried through in so many cases that I can tell within a little how long a man has been a drinker, and that with no other guide than the standard of graduated depravity which is in my mind, and which I instinctively consult. Devine must have been attractive to women, for they certainly did their best to spoil him, if one may judge by the collection of faded notes which he retains. He met his fate at last. A pretty, sentimental girl fell in love with him, and pressed him to make an appointment with her, so the dashing young actor arranged to meet the love-stricken damsel at Hampton Court. The flowers of the chestnuts were splendid, and the spirit of May was in the air. "I seem to see the same sunshine and the same flowers very often, even when I'm too jumpy to know what is going on all round," said the poor, battered man. The girl sobbed and trembled. "I couldn't help it; I had to meet you, and, Oh, if father knew, I believe he'd beat me." Devine found out that the lady was the daughter of a very rich tradesman, and he was not by any means displeased, for romantic actors have just as keen an eye to business as other folk. Before the pleasant afternoon closed, he had gained permission to call the truant Letty, and she primmed her rosy lips as he taught her to say Will. Decidedly Mr. Devine was no laggard in love.

Indiscreet little Letty found means to steal away from home time after time, and her stock of fibs must have been varied and extensive, for three months passed before the inevitable catastrophe came.

"This is Aunt Lizer, is it?"

Devine and Miss Letty were walking in a secluded corner of Wimbledon Common when a loud voice spoke thus. Letty screamed, and turned to face a stout, red-faced man who stood glaring ominously.

Devine, after the approved stage fashion, said "May I ask the meaning of this intrusion?"

"Meanin'! You talk about meanin' to John Billiter? See this stick? I'll meanin' you! This is my daughter, and I'll thank you to tell me who *you* are." Need I say that Devine rose to the occasion? He recited to me a portion of the reply which he made to the aggrieved parent, and I can fully believe that that worthy man was surprised. "The Rivals," "The Hunchback," "Romeo and Juliet," and other dramatic works were ransacked for phrases, and the stately periods flowed on until Mr. Billiter gasped, "Damn it, gal!—do you mean to say you've deceived your father so you might git out along of a blanked lunatic?" This was too much. Devine observed with majesty, "Sir, I can pardon much to the father of the lady whom I love; but there are limits, sir. Beware!"

"You come along to the trap, you hussy; and as for you mister, let me ketch you anywhere near our place and I'll turn the yard dog out on you!"

Poor Letty was severely shut up at home. Her father questioned her much, and when he heard at length that the flashy young man was an actor, he gave one choking yell, and sat down in limp fashion. All the rest of the day he muttered at intervals, "A hactor!" and pressed his hand to his forehead with many groans. At night he went into Letty's room, and as he gazed on the girl's worn face he said, "A hactor! The Billiters is done for. Their goose is cooked!"

Devine fairly luxuriated in his desolation. I could tell from his mode of dwelling on his woes that he had keenly enjoyed playing the forlorn lover. As he told me of those sleepless nights spent long ago, and rolled out his sonorous record of suffering, his watering eye gleamed with pleasure, and I can well imagine how sorely he bored his friends when he was young and his grief was at its most enjoyable height. But he was no milksop, and he resolved that Mr. Billiter should not baulk him. Where is the actor who does not delight in stratagems and mysteries? Bless their honest hearts, they could not endure life without an occasional plot or mystification! Two months after Letty's incarceration, a decently-dressed man called at Mr. Billiter's with a parcel. The visitor was clad in tweed; his smart whiskers were dexterously trained and he looked like a natty draper's assistant. "These things were ordered by post, and I wish Miss Billiter to select her own patterns."

"Miss Billiter's with her aunt, and she don't see anyone at present."

"Then kindly hand in the parcel, and I will call in an hour."

That night Letty was restless. The sly little thing had managed to deceive her aunt; but the problem of how to elude father was troublesome.

William had an American engagement; he would have a fast horse ready next evening at eight; Mr. Billiter would be summoned by a telegram; then train to Southampton—licence—the mail to New York, and bliss for ever! Letty must rush out like a truant schoolgirl—never mind about hat or cloak; the escape *must* be made, and then let those catch who can.

This was Devine's plan, and he carried it out with perfect nerve. A fortnight afterwards the mail steamer was surging along in mid-Atlantic, and the plucky actor was passing happy, idle days with his wife.

* * * * *

Billy had the nerve of a man once, but he utters a kind of strangled shriek now if a dog barks close to him, and he cannot lift his glass in the mornings—he stoops to the counter and sucks his first mouthfuls like a horse drinking, or he passes his handkerchief round his neck, and draws his liquor gently up with the handkerchief to steady him. A long way has Billy travelled since he was a merry young player. I shall say more about him presently.

THE PINK TOM CAT.

My friend the publisher calls the Loafer's narratives "thrilling," but I, as editor of the Diaries, would prefer another adjective. The Loafer was a man who only cared for gloom and squalor after he had given up the world of gaiety and refinement. Men of his stamp, when they receive a crushing mental blow, always shrink away like wounded animals and forsake their companions. A very distinguished man, who is now living, disappeared for fifteen years, and chose on his return to be regarded as an utter stranger. His former self had died, and he was strengthened and embittered by suffering. The Loafer was of that breed.

Two locked volumes of the Loafer's Diary were delivered to me, and I found that the man had once been joyous to the last degree, ambitious, successful, and full of generous thoughts and fine aspirations. Some of his songs breathe the very spirit of delight, and he wrote his glad thoughts at night when he could not sleep for the keen pleasure of living. Then comes a sudden cloud, and from that time onward the Diary is bitter, brutal, and baldly descriptive of life's abominations. It would not become me to speak with certainty, but I fancy that a woman had something to do with the Loafer's wild and reckless change. He is reticent, but his poems all point in one direction. Here is a grave note of passion:—

The sombre heather framed you round,
    The starlight touched your pallid face,
You moved across the silvered ground—
    The night was happy with your grace.

The air was steeped in silver fire,
    The gorse was touched with silvern sheen;
The nightingales—the holy choir—
    Sang bridal songs for you, my queen.

But songs and starfire, pomp of night,
    Murmur of trees and Ocean's roll,
Were poor beside the blind delight—
    The Love that quivered in my soul.

Further on there is a single brief verse like a cry of rage and despair:—

And is it then the End of all?
    O, Father! What a doom is mine—
An unreturning prodigal,
    Who feeds on husks and herds with swine!

After many ravings the torn soul seems to grow calm, and we have this pensive and tender fragment of music:—

The dreams that fill the thoughtful night,
    All holy dreams are in the sky,
They stoop to me with viewless flight,
    And bid me wave my care goodbye.

Spread your dim wings, O sacred friends,
    Fleet softly to your starry place;
I'll meet you as my journey ends,
    When I shall crave our Master's grace.

Till I may join your shadowy band
    I'll think of things that are to be—

The far-off joy, the Unseen Land,
    The Lover I shall never see.

After this our man plunges into the slums, and we have no more poetry. One who loved him asked me to go through his journals, and nearly all I know of him is derived from them. By chance I have heard that he was passionately fond of children, but avoided women. One who knew him said that he was witty, and often strung off epigrams by the hour together, but he was always subject to fits of blind frenzy, during which his wit and his genuine sagacity left him. No one followed him to his grave; but he was visited in hospital by a tall, fair lady, who gazed on him with stern composure. He sneered even while dying. "I'm a pretty object, am I not? I was going to shake the world. Will you kiss me once?"

The tall lady stooped and kissed him; he gasped, "Thank you. It was more than I deserved. And now for the Dark."

The lady sighed a little and went away, and I think that a bunch of heather which lay on the coffin must have come from her. Anyway, that is all I know about the Loafer, and he may now tell his story of the Pink Tom Cat in his own way. You observe how drily circumstantial he is.

* * * * *

I shall not be able to go on with Billy Devine's story for some time. We have had an ugly business here, and it is now two months since I wrote a line. It was only by making special inquiry that I found how time had gone, for I have been living in a nightmare.

One fine morning I put on smart flannels and went for a scull on the river. If ever you drink too much it is best to force yourself into violent exercise at any cost, and for that reason I determined to row until the effects of a very bad night had worn off. Usually I keep myself clear of after consequences, but I had been with a keen set, and we did not go to bed at all. When we contrived to separate at 7 a.m., some of my companions began on a fresh day's drinking, but I chose to take a rest.

It was a lovely morning, and I felt like a bad sort of criminal amid the clear, splendid beauty. When the light wind struck across the surface of the river it seemed as if the water were pelted with falling jewels; the osiers bowed and sighed as the breeze ran along their tops; and, here and there, a spirt of shaken dewdrops described a flashing arc, and fell poppling into the stream. Ah! how solemnly glad and pure and radiant the great trees looked! The larks had gone wild with the joy of living, and their delicious rivalry, their ceaseless gurgle of liquid melody, seemed somehow to match the multitudinous glitter of the mighty clouds of foliage. For a man with pure palate and healthy eye the sights and sounds would have made a heaven; but my mouth was like a furnace, and my eye was fevered. Nevertheless, I managed to enjoy the sweet panorama more and more as my muscles grew tense, and I pulled on doggedly for full three hours, until I had not a dry stitch on me; then a funny little waterside inn drew my eye, and I went ashore. Bob Darbishire met me with a shout of welcome, and I wondered what brought him there. Bob did not often visit The Chequers, for he was a wealthy fellow, and he liked best to fool his time away in flash billiard-rooms; but he knew me well enough, and I was on as easy terms with him as with the costers and Rommany chals. I say *was* when I speak of him. Ah me!

Bob succeeded to a great deal of ready money and a good business when he was barely twenty-one, and he broke out into a rackety life at once, for he had been hard held in by his father and mother, and his mad activities craved for some vent. Had he been well guided he would have become a useful citizen, but he was driven with a cruel bit, and the reins were savagely jerked whenever he seemed restive. When he once was free, he set off at a wild rate down the steep that leads to perdition, and plenty of people cheered him as he flew on. It vexed me often to see a fine, generous lad surrounded by spongers who rooked him at every turn; but what could one do? The sponger has no mercy and no manliness; he is always a person with violent appetites, and he will procure excitement at the cost of his manliness and even of his honesty. Bob had an open hand, and thought nothing of paying for twenty brandies-and-sodas in the course of a morning. Twenty times eightpence does not seem much, but if you keep up that average daily for a year you have spent a fair income. No one ever tried to stay this prodigal with a word of advice; indeed, in such cases advice is always useless, for the very man whom you may seek to save is exceedingly likely to swear, or even to strike at you. He thinks you impugn his wisdom and sharpness, and he loves, above all things, to be regarded as an acute fellow. A few favoured gentry almost lived on Bob, and scores of outsiders had pretty pickings when he was in a lavish humour, which was nearly every day. He betted on races, and lost; he played billiards, and lost; he ran fox terriers, and lost; he played Nap for hours at a stretch, and generally lost. He was only successful in games that required strength and daring. Then, of course, he must needs emulate the true sporting men in amorous achievements, and thus his income bore the drain of some two or three little establishments. Bob would always try to drink twice as much as any other man, and he treated himself with the same liberality in the matter of ex-barmaids and chorus girls. The Wicked Nobleman was a somewhat reckless character in his way, but his feats would not bear comparison with those performed by many and many a young fellow who belongs to the wealthy middle class. Alas! for that splendid middle class which once represented all that was sober and steady and trustworthy in Britain! Go into any smart billiard-room nowadays, or make a round of the various race meetings, and you will see something to make you sad. You see one vast precession of Rakes making their mad Progress.

Bob was always kindly with me, as, indeed, he was with everybody. The very bookmakers scarcely had the heart to offer him false prices, and only the public-house spongers gave him no law. But, then the sponger spares nobody. On this memorable morning the lad was rigged in orthodox flannels, and he looked ruddy and well, but the ruddiness was not quite of the right sort. He had begun drinking early, and his eye had that incipient gloss which always appears about the time when the one pleasurable moment of drunkenness has come. There is but one pleasant moment in a drinking bout, and men make themselves stupid by trying to make that fleeting moment permanent. Bob cried, "Come on, sonny. Oh! what would I give for your thirst! Mine's gone! I'm three parts copped already. Come on. Soda, is it?"

Then, with the usual crass idiocy of our tribe, we proceeded to swallow oblivion by the tumbler until the afternoon was nearly gone. I felt damp and cold and sticky, so I said I should scull home and change my clothes. Then Darbishire yelled with spluttering cordiality, "Home! Not if I know it! My togs just fit you. Go and have a bath, and we'll shove you in the next room to mine. I'm on the rampage, and Joe Coney's coming tonight. You've got nothing to do. Have it out with us. Blow me! we'll have a week—we'll have a fortnight—we'll have a month."

I wish I had never taken part in that rampage.

Towards eight o'clock we both felt the false craving for food which is produced by alcohol, and we clamoured for dinner. Dinner under such circumstances produces a delusive feeling of sobriety, and men think that they have killed the alcohol; but the stuff is still there, and every molecule of it is ready, as it were, to explode and fly through the blood when a fresh draught is added. At eleven o'clock we were at cards with Mr. Coney. At one we went out to admire the moon, and though one of us saw two moons, he felt a dull pain at the heart as he remembered days long ago, when the pale splendour brought gladness. When we had solemnly decided that it was a fine night, we went back to our reeking room again, and pursued our conversation on the principle that each man should select his own subject and try to howl down the other two. This exercise soon palled on us, and one by one we sank to sleep. The clear light was pouring in when I woke, but the very sight of the straight beams made me doleful. When a man is in training, that gush of brightness makes him joyous; but a night with the fiend poisons the light, the air, the soul. Bob lay on the floor under the full glare of the window. What a fine fellow he was! His chest bulged strongly under his fleecy sweater; his neck was round and muscular, and every limb of him seemed compact and hard. His curls were all dishevelled, and his face was miserably puffy, but he had not had time to become bloated. No wonder that girls liked him.

Presently we were all awake, and a more wretched company could not very well be found. Novelists talk about "a debauch" in a way that makes novices think debauchery has something grand and mysterious about it. "We must have orgies; it's the proper thing," says Tom Sawyer the delightful. The raw lad finds "debauches" mentioned with majestic melancholy, and he naturally fancies that, although a debauch may be wicked, it is neither nasty nor contemptible. Why cannot some good man tell the sordid truth? I suppose he would be accused of Zolaism, but he would frighten away many a nice lad from the wrong road. Let any youngster who reads this try to remember his worst sick headache; let him (if he has been to sea) remember that moment when he longed for someone to come and throw him overboard; let him then imagine that he has committed a deadly crime; let him also fancy what he would feel if he knew that some awful irreparable calamity must inevitably fall on him within an hour. Then he will understand that state of mind and body which makes men loathe beauty, loathe goodness, loathe life; then he will understand what jolly fellows endure.

We glowered glassily on each other, and we were quite ready either to quarrel or to shed tears on the faintest provocation. Presently Bob laughed in a forced way, and said, "God, what a head! Let's come out. Those yellow shades make me bilious." The glory of full day flooded the lovely banks, but the light pained our eyes, and we sought refuge in the cool, dim shades of the parlour. Our conversation was exactly like that of passengers on board ship when they are just about to collapse. The minutes seemed like hours; our limbs were listless, as if we had been beaten into helplessness. So passed one doleful hour. I mentioned breakfast, and Bob shuddered, while Coney rushed from the room. What a pleasant thing is a jovial night!

"Let's see if we can manage some champagne," said Darbishire, and the "merry" three were soon mournfully gazing on a costly magnum. Sip by sip we contrived to drink a glass each; then the false thirst woke, the nausea departed, and we were started again for the day.

I persisted in taking violent exercise, but Darbishire seemed to have lost all his muscular aptitudes, and although I implored him to exert himself, he sank into a lethargy that was only varied by mad fits, during which he performed the freaks of a lunatic. After the sixth day's drinking I proposed to go away. Bob looked queerly at me, and said in a whisper, "Don't you try it on! See that!" and he showed me a little Derringer. I laughed; but I was not really amused. You always notice that, when a man is about to go wrong, he thinks of killing those whom he likes best. That night Bob's hands flew asunder with a jerk while we were playing cards; the cards flew about; then he flung a decanter violently into the fireplace, and sat down trembling and glaring. I sprang to his side, and found that the sweat was running down his neck. I pulled off his shoes—his socks were drenched! I said, "I thought you'd get them, old fellow. Now, have some beef-tea, and I'll send right away for a sleeping draught." Bob trembled still more.

"No beef-tea. I've had nothing these three days, as you know. It would kill me to swallow." Then he said, in a horrible whisper, "The brute's coming down the chimney again. There's a paw! Now his head! Now's a chance! Yah! you pink devil, that's got you! Three days you've been coming, and now you're cheeky. Yeo, ho! That's done him." Then he flung a second decanter, and sank down once more with a shriek.

"I'll have a drink on that!" he screamed; and I let him take a full glass of spirits, for I wanted to secure the Derringer. The drink appeared to paralyse him, and I slipped down to the landlord's room. The worthy man took things very coolly; none of his trade ever like to see a man drunk, but they become hardened to it in time, and talk about delirium tremens as if it were measles. Here is the dialogue.

"Bob's queer."

"I thought so. He's had 'em once before. He must be careful, but you can't stop him."

"I must have help. I could drown myself when I think that I've perhaps encouraged him."

"Don't you worry yourself. He'd have been a million times worse if you'd not been about. He sits with the watchmen and all sorts of tow-rags then."

"We must get him home somehow."

The landlord fairly shouted: "Home! anything but that! Not that I want to keep him, but we must have him right first. There's his mother, what could she do?" Then, dropping his voice, the shrewd fellow said, "You see, it would nearly pay me to be without his custom, for I'm in the old lady's hands. Fact is, they've engaged him to a swell girl, and she's awful spoons on him, for there ain't nobody so nice and hearty as he is when he's square. He's fond of her, too, but she wants to *reclaim* him, don't you know, and he kinder kicks. So he says when he came, "I'm going to be out of apron-strings for a bit," and I don't want him to go near home till he's fit to meet the lady. She's a screamer, she is—a real swell; and she'd go off her head if she saw him with 'em on. I'll tell you what we'll do. I've got one bromide of potass draught. We'll get that into him somehow, and in the morning we may manage to feed him. During the day we'll get some more stuff from the doctor, and patch him up ready for home I don't care to see him again, for there's no stopping him."

When I went up to our room, Bob was lying on the floor, and breathing heavily. He opened his eyes, rose, and staggered a little; then he said, "B'lieve I can walk a bit; come out for a stroll on the tow-path." The moon was charging through wild clouds, and the river was flecked alternately by strong lights and broad swathes of shadow. Bob muttered as he walked; so, to give him an excuse for conversation, I said, "Why were you chucking the hardware so gay and free, Robert?" He put his lips to my ear, and said, "That pink tom cat has followed me for ever so long, and I can't do for him anyhow. By God, he's everywhere! A pink cat, you know, with eyes made of red fire. He's on to me just when I don't expect him. Take me for a row. The brute can't come on the water."

"You'll never go out tonight!"

"Won't I? And so will you, or I'll know the reason why!"

I had not secured that Derringer.

I picked a big, broad boat at the inn stairs, and we were soon dropping gently over the tide, but I would not row hard, as I wanted to be near assistance. To my astonishment Darbishire began to talk quite lucidly, and went on for a few minutes with all the charm that distinguished him when he was sober. By some strange process the blood had begun to circulate with regularity in the vessels of the impoverished brain, and the man was sane. I was overjoyed, and in the fulness of my heart I said, "We'll drive home, or row there tomorrow. My dear fellow, I thought you were going dotty." His jaw fell; he yelled, "Stop him—stop him! He's coming with his mouth open! Oh! red-hot teeth and his belly full of flames—the cat! Oh, I'll stand this no more—you brute, you shall drown!" In an instant he sprang overboard; the clouds came over the moon, and I could only tell Bob's whereabouts by hearing him wallowing and snarling like a dog. I backed up to him, leaned over, and passed one of the rudder-lines under his arm-pits; his struggling ceased and I shouted for help. Lights moved on the bank, and presently a boat shot towards us. The landlord said, "Mercy on us! Excuse me, sir, but you did ought to be careful. You ought to be shot for risking that man's life; I see as how it is." I was only too glad to have missed seeing a tragedy, and I let Boniface talk on.

It was agreed that Bob should have his draught, and that I should sit up by his bedside till four next morning. We wrapped him in warm blankets, and coaxed him into taking the medicine. He started and twitched for some time, and at last sank into sleep. He moaned again and again, but showed no signs of waking, and I sat quietly smoking and framing good resolutions. My eyeballs were irritable, and I found that I could only obtain ease by closing my eyes. Once I started up and walked to and fro; then it struck me I ought to throw the Derringer out of the window, and I did so; then I sat down. The clock struck two; my tired eyes closed, but I was sure I could keep awake, and I began to repeat old songs merely to test my memory and keep the brain active.

Crash! I was sitting on the floor. The clock struck one, two, three! Bob was gone. I had fallen asleep and betrayed my trust. I could have cried, but that would do little good. The door opened, and Darbishire appeared—prowling stealthily and glaring. A long glitter met my eye, and I saw that Bob had taken down an old Yeomanry sabre from the wall of the next room. He came on, and I shrank under the shadow of my arm-chair. He heaved up the sabre, and shouted, "Now, you beast, I've got you on the hop!" and hacked at the bed with wild fury. As he turned his back on me, I prepared to lay hold on him; he whirled round swiftly, and my heart came into my mouth. I cried out, "Bob, old man!" He started furiously for a second, and then made a pass at me, sending the steel through my clothes on the right side. I felt a slight sting, but did not mind, and by wrenching myself half round I tore the sabre from his hand. Then I closed, and held him, in spite of his struggles and frothing curses, until the landlord and ostler burst in and helped me.

The cut on my side only needed sticking-plaister, but I was completely exhausted, and I resolved not to risk such another experience for any price. I said to the landlord, "He must be taken to the town, where we can have a doctor and attendants handy."

"But you won't drive that poor lady out of her senses, will you?"

"No, I'll take him to The Chequers, and smuggle him in at night. They know me there, and not a soul but the doctor and the men will be able to tell where he is."

Boniface was not quite satisfied, but he agreed to lend me two men, and at dusk I drove round to the back gate of The Chequers, and smuggled Bob through the stables.

He was very well behaved when the doctor came, and even thanked him for providing two careful attendants. The doctor's directions were very simple. "I'll give him some strong meat essence at once; then he must have the draught that I will send. No alcohol on any consideration, no matter if he goes on his knees to you. Let him have milk and beef-tea as often as you can, and never leave him for an instant."

Our landlord of The Chequers was very funny about the jim-jams, and funnier still about my suddenly taking to swell company; but I let him talk on, and he certainly kept unusually quiet, though no more inveterate gossip ever lived.

At a very late hour I was strolling homeward, long after the last reeling coster had swayed and howled towards his slum, when two women stopped me Then a man came from the shadow of the wall, and I thought I had fallen across some strange night-birds; but one of the women spoke, and I knew she was a lady. "You have my boy in that horrid place. Tell me, is he well? I must see him; I'll tear the doors down with my nails." Then the man said, "I drove the keb, sir. I knows Mr. Robert, and I thought I'd better tell his mother." I eagerly said, "Madam, you shall see him, but, pray, not tonight. The shock might kill him. On my honour he is in good hands, and I promise to come to you on the instant when it is safe for you to meet him." The lady moaned, "Oh, my boy—my darling—my own! Oh! the curse!"—and then she went away.

In two days Bob was quite calm and rational. He craved for food, and seemed so well that I thought I might manage him single-handed. So the attendants were dismissed, with the doctor's permission, and Bob and I settled down for a quiet chat. I shall never forget that talk. The lad was not maudlin, and he utterly refused to whimper, but he seemed suddenly to have seen the horror of the past. "You can stop in time, old man," he said, "but I can't. When I'm well, I'll turn to work, and I'll try to keep other chaps from getting into the mud. It would be funny to see me preaching to the boys up river, wouldn't it?" For a moment I thought, "I'll turn teetotal as well," but I did not say it. I bent towards Bob and asked,

"Would you care to see your mother, old man?" He smiled beautifully, and eagerly answered, "Go for her now."

I was away about two hours, and returned with Mrs. Darbishire. The landlord met us, and gravely said "I've been away, but the potman tells me a queer yarn. Mr. Darbishire made queer signs out of window to the man you call the Ramper, and Mr. Ramper goes to the pub over the way and then up to the room. And now Mr. Robert's been locked in for a hour and a half." My heart gave one leap, and then I felt cold. We hurried up stairs, and we heard a long shrill snarl—not like a human voice.

"Locked! Fetch a crowbar, and call up one of the lads to help."

We burst open the door, and there on the bed lay Bob. He was chattering, as it were, in his sleep, and a brandy bottle lay on the floor. He had swallowed nearly the whole of the poison raw, and his limbs were paralyzed. Suddenly he opened his eyes; then he writhed and yelled, "Mother!—the beast! the beast!" The lady threw herself down on her knees with a pitiful cry, but Bob did not speak to her. He never spoke any more.

TEDDY.

I was so weak and nervous after Bob Darbishire's death that I did not go much to The Chequers; I hid myself most in my own rooms. The funeral was attended by all the well-to-do folks in the district; but I was not there, because I did not care to pass by The Chequers in the procession. Most people had a good word for poor Bob, and many kind fellows could not mention him without the tears coming into their eyes. Only the spongers were indifferent; but they had, of course, to look around for another liberal spendthrift. Bob was so young, and bright, and brave; I never knew a straighter or a kinder man, and I have seen few who had so much ability. He drifted into drunkenness by accident, and the vice had him hard by the throat before he found out that he was really a prisoner. He struggled for awhile, and repented again and again; but his will was captured, and when once a man's will is enslaved, vices seem to come easy to him. I am not fit to moralise about his relations with women; I only know that he was a sinner, and I think of his temptations. Like so many splendid young Englishmen, he was conquered by drink. The vice seizes on some of the best in all classes, and the finest flowers soon become as worthless as weeds when the blight has caught them. It is nearly always the bright lad of a family, the most promising, the mother's darling, that goes wrong; it is the brilliant students, the men of whom one says, "Ah, what could he not do if he would only try!" is those who trip, and quench their brilliance in the mud. A little rift in the fabric of the will, a little instability of temper, an unlucky week of idleness— these are the things that start a man towards the very gulf of doom. Bob Darbishire, the athlete, the delightful and exhilarating companion, was set gliding on the slope, and now he and his hopes and his unknown capabilities have passed away, deeper than ever plummet sounded. It is a big puzzle. I am a loafer, and I suppose I shall never be anything else, so it is not for me to solve the ugly problem.

The Ramper fawned on me, and asked me if I had heard of "that there pore young bloke wot kicked the bucket upstairs."

I said, "Yes; I fancy he was murdered. Do you know who took the brandy up to him?"

The Ramper looked very wicked, but merely answered, "'Ow should I know? He arst me, and I goes and says, 'No, sir; not for a thick 'un.' I see 'ow he was. I've 'ad 'em on myself, and I knowed as 'ow he wasn't up there for nothing."

The Ramper is undoubtedly a liar.

The Wanderer often asked me to call, for he knows that I have a stiff flask in my pocket every night. I have pieced out the rest of his story, and I shall put it into my book when I am less glum. At present I swear every day that I shall turn temperance lecturer, and spend my money on the Cause; but, somehow, habit, and my roving blood, are too much for me. Like all men of my sort, from Burns downward, I can see evils clearly, and state their nature plainly enough; but when it comes to keeping clear of them, I resemble my tribe in being rather unhandy at judicious strategy. *Vogue la galére!*

Three months more have gone and my journals have never been written up, save in chance scraps. The Wanderer is quite as interesting as ever! I took the odds to £2 with him over a race run at Newmarket, and he paid promptly. He puts out little signs of improvement—sprouts of gentility—at times: but one heavy spell of gin and Shakespeare takes him back to the old level again. Still, he is more amusing than the dandies; in fact, I do not think I shall go amongst the respectable division again. I make no pretence of immolating myself: I go among the blackguards and wastrels because I am fascinated; I tell exactly what I see, and leave other people to make practical use of my words. During the last three months

I have been, as usual, hard hit. It seems as though any creature that I am fond of must soon be lost to me, and the pages of my journal are like rows of tombstones.

We were making a great noise in the bar one night, for a cornet and fiddle were playing, and a few couples were moved by the music and the beer to begin dancing. A good many women come in at one time or other, and their shrill laughter forms the treble of our crashing chorus. One tall, broad-shouldered dame, who boasts of having six sons serving in the Guards, made a great commotion. Her weight is considerable. She had been drinking for four hours, and, when she attempted to illustrate her theory of the waltz, she sent drinkers and drink flying as though her offspring's battalion had charged. She had disabled one sporting coster who tried to guide her, and the landlord was preparing for practical remonstrance, when she sailed down upon me, yawing all the way as though she were running before a hard breeze. I prepared for the shock, but I was not destined to receive it. A tiny little lad had just received some beer in a bottle from the counter, and he was making for home, when the tall woman plumped upon him. The bottle was broken, the beer ran among the dirt and sawdust, and the little lad was almost smothered before the landlord (who impolitely addressed the waltzer as a cow) had managed to haul the ponderous woman to her feet. The boy was a good deal hurt physically, but his mental distress at sight of the lost beer prevented him from noticing his bruises. When he fully grasped the extent of the calamity he actually became pale, and I do not think I ever saw such a piteous little face in my life. I asked "How much was it, little 'un?" His lips trembled, and he said, "I dunno. I put a-money down, and her knows what to put in a-bottle. Father got to 'ave his beer, else he not have good supper." I thought, "This youngster isn't ill-used, or he wouldn't be anxious for his father to have a good supper." Then I ordered a pint can of ale, and offered it to the youth. He hesitated, and said, "It's dark. I slip on a stone, and then more beer gone," so I took his hand, and marched off with the can, notwithstanding the fact that my

39

friend the cornet player struck up "See the conquering hero" in a most humorous and embarrassing manner.

It was very quiet and fresh outside, after the hoarse wrangling and the dreadful air, and I liked to have the boy's soft hand in mine. He said, "Missa Benjo's cellar open. Two mens fall down a-night; you keep a-hold o' my hand." I went very warily down the alley, and found that Mr. Benjo had assuredly left an awkward trap for the people from The Chequers. My young man seemed very smart and careful, and he soon led to a lone door which opened into a den that was half kitchen, half cellar.

"Who a-you got long o' you, Teddy?" inquired a gruff man who was crouched on a stool by the side of the empty grate.

"It's a man, father, wot give me the beer."

"Come in, mate, if you've a mind."

I accepted the invitation, prompted by my usual curiosity, and found myself in a stinking little box, which was lit by a guttering dip. Some clothes hung on a line, and these offended more senses than one. No breath of pure air seemed to have blown through that gruesome dwelling for many a day, but I am seasoned, and nothing puts me out much.

"Ain't got another seat, mate. Take the bed."

The bed was not suggestive of sleep, and I was a trifle uneasy as I sat down; yet I knew it would never do to hesitate, so down I sat.

"Wot's this about givin' Teddy the beer?"

I made answer.

"Ain't got no more 'n two bloomin' dee, but you can have 'em, and thank ye for your trouble."

"I have money enough, thanks. A pint isn't much."

"Oh, now I knows you. A bloke was a-tellin' me they had a broken-down toff round at The Chequers, and some on 'em says you ain't no more broken down 'n the Lord Mayor. Allus got enough for a 'eavy booze. Anyway, you talks like a toff. I used to git round to the bar, but it don't run to it now. Two kids; and Teddy's clothes there ain't not so easy to buy now. Missus is out charin'. She'll fetch us a bit o' supper, and I makes out middlin' well along o' my pint and bit o' bacca. How's things, mate?"

I said that things were flourishing fairly.

"You ain't never done much blank work, *you* ain't. Your dukes is same as silk. Bin a tailor?"

"No, I have other work to do."

"All square, mate; 'tain't no business o' mine. Things is bad 'ere. The blank, blank swine of a blank landlord, he takes pooty well 'alf of every tanner I can make, and d—d if he'll do anything to the place."

"Smells are queer down here."

"Smell! Lord love you, come down yere to-morrer, and you'll git to know wot stinks is. Let Teddy show you that 'ere bloomin' ditch at the back. They calls it a stream, but I dussn't say wot I thinks it is afore the nipper. All the dead cats and muck in the bloomin' crehation gits dumped in there. On 'ot days you wants a nosebag on, I tell you, and no error."

"Does Teddy go to school?"

"No fear; not yet. But he's fly as they makes 'em, he is. Useful he is, too. 'Andy as makes no matter, and he ain't no more 'n seven."

"Well, I'm coming to see Teddy and the ditch tomorrow. Will you have another pint?"

"Right, matey; that'll do for tomorrow. Ain't you got no less 'n a tanner? Never mind, I'll square when I'm flush."

Next day I visited the alley, and went to the gap where it opened on to the ditch. There was an admirably efficient hotbed for rearing diseases there. A solid bed of sewage of about two feet deep seemed to fill the hollow, and a thin sheet of filthy water covered this bed—with sickly breaks here and there. Ordure palpable and abominable was plentiful, and the swollen carcasses of small animals exhaled their biting wafts. Poor little Teddy! I said, "Come home with me, will you? Mind, you mustn't tell anyone where I live;" and the amiable little dot set off at my side. He could not walk very well, for he had one shoe minus a sole, and his toes stuck through the other. When we reached my room I sent out for a pair of boots and two pairs of socks; then I pitched Teddy's away, and presently to his terror, and my own amusement, I found myself engaged in washing his feet. Nice little feet they were when they came clean, and their owner pattered about with perfect satisfaction on my carpet. I pulled out some cakes, and Teddy accepted a few, turning away his head as he took them. He had the exact look of a dog that is being reproved, and I had some trouble in persuading him to begin. When he had finished one sponge-cake he grinned and enigmatically observed, "Teddy's belly." I said, "That's baby talk. You talked all right last night. Finish your cakes and you'll have some more for tea. Trot about as you like till it's ready." He went gaily about, touching some articles, and even sniffing at others; he dived into my bedroom, and I heard him cry "Ooh!" Then there was a scraping sound, and Teddy appeared lugging a small looking-glass and smiling broadly. "Ooh! This is what there is when a lady gives you a beer." I understood that he referred to the bleared glass behind the bar of the Chequers, and I appreciated Teddy's powers of comparison; but I explained to him that mirrors cannot be safely hauled about by little boys, and he kindly assented to this proposition.

We had tea, and Teddy so far improved on his bashfulness that he made grabs at several things which would have disagreed with him if I had let him follow his inclinations. He affably received my hints on table etiquette, and smiled with gentleness when I told him he had eaten enough. The little creature's ideas were like those of a dog. He had been taught to follow and to come home to his kennel; he was ready to be gracious toward those who fed him, and he had the true canine glance which expresses gratitude and expectancy at once. But he was only a rudimentary human being, and his brain power had slept so far. I showed him Caldecott's wonderful "House that Jack Built," and he gloated over that delightful villain of a dog; the cat and the rat he understood, but he knew nothing of the cow. I let him stare at the dog as long as he chose, and he chuckled like a magpie all the time. He proposed to remove the picture-book, and it was only with difficulty that I persuaded him to let me keep it. Knowing the street arab class very well, I did not try to talk with him, for I have always found that an arab's curiosity when he finds himself in a new place renders him incapable of attending to anything that is said to him until he has learned the appearance of every object in the room. The little chap is a barbarian, and you must treat him exactly as you would treat an adult member of a friendly savage tribe.

Before Teddy went home I rigged him up in his new boots and stockings, and he was amusingly proud. When we parted at the alley he said, "You let me go you house again, and have some nice things and see the dog?" Of course I invited him, and henceforth he waylaid me in the afternoons as I went home. At first he was not polite, and his mode of calling, "Hoy, man! wait for me!" drew marked attention from the public. But he soon learned to lift his hat and to shake hands. At intervals I gave him set lessons on manners, and, if he behaved nicely, we had a game at cricket in my queer old garden. It was almost impossible to make Teddy understand the morality of any game at first. When he learned that the ball must not touch his wicket, his treatment of my slow bowling was positively immoral. I did not mind his kicking the ball out of the way, nor did I object to his using his bat like a scoop; but when he lay down in front of the wicket, and sweetly smiled as the ball touched his stomach, I had to insist on severe cricketing etiquette. As the nights darkened in I took to amusing myself more and more with Teddy, and sometimes I did not go out to the Chequers at all. The boy was a severe trial to me when he learned to play draughts. When once the fundamental laws of the game dawned on his mind, and he understood that he must try to reduce the number of my pieces, he thought that any means were justified if he could be successful. Once I left the room for a minute while we were playing, and on my return found four of my men had disappeared. I said, "Where are those men?" Teddy smiled courteously; "I taken 'em. I go hop, hop, hop, over a lot. All fair." "But where have you put them?" "In a pocket. All fair." But he gradually grew out of his habits of picking and stealing, and he behaved much like a well-trained dog. It is plain to me that he regarded me as a sort of deity; but his love was quite unalloyed by fear. He would stroke my beard, and say, "You very nice," when I had been specially good-humoured, and, as his stock of words increased, he prattled on by the hour. One must love something, and I got into the habit of loving this pale little urchin, so that at length I fitted up a crib for him, and asked his mother to let him stay with me. This made a great change in my habits. Teddy seemed to wake as by magic, if I rose to go out after he was in bed, and, although he never cried, his way of saying, "You won't let me stop by myself—perhaps the black man might come," always settled me. By degrees I fell into the habit of reading at nights, and the steady life made my brain clear. Books that had been dim memories to me for years became vivid, and the power of sustained thinking came back. In those long, calm evenings, I went through my Gibbon again, and the awful pageant that rolls past our view under the direction of the aristocrat of literature made my late life seem poor and mean. How low we were! The darkened costers are interesting as studies in animal life; but the more pretentious persons whose humour reaches its highest flight in an indecent story, and whose wit consists in calling someone else a liar—how petty they are, and how fruitless is their friendship! I began to feel like a patrician who surveys the mob from his lordly dais, and I almost resolved to go back to the clubs and theatres once more.

Teddy increased so much in mental power that he took interest in fairy tales, and he was a rigorous taskmaster. I was obliged to illustrate the stories in varied ways. Once I was asked, "What's a gian'?" I said, "A very, very big man." "Big as you?" "Far bigger." "How bigger? Has he got legs, and heads, and—and things like that?" "We'll see. When I stand on this chair I'm as big as a giant," but it was all of no avail, and only after Teddy had seen a huge, knock-kneed being in a penny show did he understand what a giant could be like. Then he asked for giant stories on all occasions.

It struck me that I was neglecting Teddy's religious education. Hundreds and thousands of such little fellows in and about London have no notion of a God, or any ruling power save the policeman. I had a dark mind to deal with, and Teddy's questions fairly beat me. Of course I took the old orthodox ideas, and tried to make them simple, but Teddy posed me like this:

"Do God live in a sky?"

"Far away. Yes; well, say in the sky."

"Where does he hang up his coat when he goes to his bed?"

What on earth was a poor, distracted loafer to say? I could not deal with Jesus, for I saw that Teddy did not understand goodness. He knew that I was kind, and he liked to kiss my hand slily, and rub his cheek on my knee; but abstract goodness and gentle words like those of Jesus did not appeal to him. I was satisfied to have a queer creature that followed me like a dog, and I am afraid that if he had lived I should have made him a kind of heathen; but the luck was against me. Teddy's father came on a Sunday morning, and said, "If you don't mind, his mother'd like to 'ave him along to dinner tomorrow. We got a bit o' pork and a horrange spesshal for him." So Teddy went home when the ditch was in worse order than usual. He had been kept amid good air, and he was clean—I washed him myself—and I fancy that the stenches poisoned him simply because he could not become acclimatised to the alley again. Anyway, he was heavy and listless when he came back, and in two days I had to send for his father and mother. I am not going into any pathetic details, for that is not my line. Night after night I walked the floor with the youngster, and when the doctor said I should catch diphtheria if I kissed him, I said I didn't care a damn, for I was wild. Then my boy went away.

One night I was walking about the park in mad fashion while a hoarse gale roused a deep chorus among the trees. I could have sworn that my lad called to me. Then I went back and dropped into The Chequers. The Ramper said, "Wot cher, yer old bugaboo?" The Wanderer shouted, "Now let the trumpet to the kettle speak; the kettle to the cannoneer without. He comes! He comes!"

And I went home and stayed till dawn with the Wanderer. That is the way we live.

THE WANDERER AGAIN.

Several racing men have warned me against the Wanderer, in their peculiarly friendly way. They want me to bet with *them*. But I like the Bohemian, the blackleg, better than I do better men. Moreover, though I am carefully informed that he is a blackleg, I find him honest. His story has long been hanging in my mind, and we may as well take it at once.

Devine's runaway match turned out well for a time. When old Mr. Billiter came home and heard what had happened he fell in a fit, and, on his recovery, he went about for a long time moaning, "We'll never hold up our heads no more." His friends thought he would lose his reason, for he would stop people in the street, and say, "Have you a daughter? Kill her, if you care for her. Mine's gone off with a hactor." But the young couple were happy enough in reality, and Devine took the fancy of the New Yorkers to such a degree that his engagement was extended over three years. Letty Devine led a gay, careless life; her husband had plenty of money, and she was introduced to pleasures that made the frowsy life of home seem very repulsive. Devine was kind to her, and continued to play the lover in his pompous style. She was proud of her man, too. He played Claude Melnotte for his benefit once, and she longed to say to the ladies in the theatre, "He belongs to me. How could she help being fascinated with him? Where could you find such another princely being?" She felt a lump in her throat when the great house rose at her William, and the more so since she knew that her praise was more to him than all the clamour of the theatre. Devine had begun by fortune-hunting, and ended by loving his wife, though she did not bring him a penny.

Those were merry days in New York. Champagne was plentiful as water, and William Devine often came home in a very lively condition, but his wife did not mind, for she thought that a man must have his glass. Women of the lower and middle classes have a great deal to do with supplying customers to the public-house. Some of them drive their men there by nagging, but more of them lead a man on to drink by sheer indulgence. They encourage him to enjoy himself without thinking of the day when enjoyment will be impossible, and when they and their children will reach the lowermost rung of the ladder of shame and penury. The Wanderer went merrily on his way, but his vice was steadily gaining on him, and his nerve was going. He took a long engagement for an Australian tour, and carried on very loosely all the while; but Letty saw no change. Women never do until the very worst has happened. When Devine came to England he was eagerly looked after, and he should have fared well. For a time he had engagements and money in plenty, but a subtle change was taking place in him, and managers and audiences saw it, though they could not say precisely where the deterioration had taken place.

There is a certain sporting set of theatrical men who are very dangerous companions. Their daily work is exciting, and when they want change they often gamble, because that is the only form of excitement which is keener than the stir and tumult of the theatre. When Devine won three hundred pounds on one Derby he was a lost man. He pitted his wits against the bookmakers'; he took to loafing about with those flash, cunning fellows who appear to spend their mornings in bars and their evenings in music-halls; he lost his ambition, and he began to lead a double life. In the end he took to presenting himself at the theatre in various stages of drunkenness, and on one unlucky night he practically settled his own fate by falling down on the stage after he had blundered over his lines a dozen times. The public saw little of him after that, for he had not the power of Kean, or Cooke, or Brooke.

They all go the same way when they slip as Devine did. You can meet them on the roads, in common lodging-houses, in the workhouse. The residuum is constantly recruited from the "comfortable" classes, and, out of thousands of cases, I never knew half-a-dozen in which the cause was not drink. I blame nobody. A drunkard is always selfish—the most selfish of created beings—and his flashes of generosity are symptoms of disease. If he lives to be cured of his vice his selfishness disappears, and he is another man; but so long as he is mastered by the craving, all things on earth are blotted out for him saving his own miserable personality. So far does the disease of egotism go, that it is impossible to find a drunkard who can so much as listen to another person; he is inexorably impelled to utter forth *his* views with more or less incoherence.

Devine, the tender husband, the kind father, became a mere slinker, a haunter of tap-rooms, a weed. Sometimes he was lucky enough to win a pound or two on a race, and that was his only means of support. The children were ragged; Letty tried to live on tea and bread, but the lack of food soon brought her low, and from sheer weakness she became a pitiful slattern.

Mr. Billiter was informed that a woman "like a beggar" wanted to see him particularly. He was about to order her off at first, but he finished by going to the door, and the beggar-woman went on her knees to him. He trembled; then he fairly lifted the poor soul up in his arms and sobbed hard. "My gal, my pooty as was. My little gal. To think as you never come before you was like this. I've bin dead since you was away. My 'art was dead, my little gal. And you're goin' away no more, never no more, with no hactors. Sit down. Give me that shawl. Lord bless me, it's a dish clout! And your neck's like a chicken's, and your breasts is all flat, as was round as could be. O me!"

But the good fellow's moanings soon fell on deaf ears, for Letty fainted. When she came round, the servants fed her, and she began to cry for the children. "Children if you like, but never him," said Billiter; and he at once drove off to bring his darling's ragged little ones home.

Devine was snoring on the floor when the old tradesman entered the lodging. There was no fire, no furniture, no food, and the half-naked children were huddled together for warmth. The youngest two screamed when a rough man came in, for they thought it was the brokers once more. Billiter sent the eldest out for a candle, which he stuck in an empty gin-bottle. He looked at the snoring drunkard, and gave him a contemptuous push with his foot; but the one little boy screamed, "You not touch my dada, you bad man!" and the old fellow was instantly ashamed. He said, "Now, my little dears, I want you to come to your mamma. She sent me for you. We'll all go away in a warm carriage, and you'll have something warm and nice to eat. Put the youngsters' clothes on, my gal."

"We've none of us got any clothes, sir."

"My God! Here, you sir—wake up. Sit against the wall. Do you see me? I've got your wife at home, and I'm going to take these kids. You'll hear from me tomorrow."

"Devine finally woke just before the public-houses closed. He staggered out, and, after his first drink, the memory of what had passed flashed back on him. He felt in his pockets. Yes! He had some money—a good deal as it happened, for he had put five shillings on a horse at 33 to 1. "Pull yourself together, Billy," he muttered. "You must have a warm bed tonight, and face it out tomorrow. One more drink, and I'll have my bed here."

In the morning he felt wretched, but when he had regained his nerve by the usual method he acted like a man. First he wrote a letter to his wife. (I saw the yellow old copy of it.)

"Dearest,—I had a bit of luck yesterday, and took too much on the strength of it. I was carried home from this house, and I could not speak to Lily or any of them. I deserve to lose you, and I will never ask you to come back unless there is no fear of more misery. But this I will do. I intend to maintain my own children, if I go and sell matches. I won eight pounds odd yesterday. I squandered one pound, I keep two to make a fresh start, and you have the rest. While this heart shall beat—yes, while memory holds her seat, as the poet says, you are dear to me. Once more, in the poet's words, I grapple you to my soul with hoops of steel. What has come over me I do not know, and when I wake to the fact of my degradation I go madly to the drink again. But I will try, and I implore your forgiveness. I cannot hope to see you often, and it is better that I should not, for I am worthless. But think of me, and, if I fall again and again, believe me that I shall go on striving to do better.—Until death, I am your loving, W. DEVINE."

"We don't want none of his 'oss-racin' money. Send it back, my gal," growled old Billiter when he saw this letter. But the poor woman would not hurt her husband.

Devine found all respectable employments closed to him, and he was often in desperate straits; but he would always contrive to send something, if it were only a half-crown, toward the support of his children. When he reached the Nadir of shabbiness, he touted in Piccadilly among the cabs, and picked up a few coppers in that way. For days he could abstain from drink, but that curse never left him, and he broke down again and again, only to repent and strive more fervently than ever. Alas! how weak we are. Surely we should help each other. I am often tempted to forget there is evil in the world. There are moments when I can almost pardon myself, but that is too hard. Devine said he could not see Letty often. He only saw her once more. She was ailing and weakly, and one day she put her arms round her father's neck, and whispered to him. He started, and growled, "All right, my gal; I deny you nothin'. Only I'll go out of the 'ouse before he comes."

So William Devine was summoned, and he found his wife propped up in bed. Her hands were frail, and the bones of her arms stood out sharply. The man was choking, Letty made an effort, lifted her arms, and drew him down to her with an ineffable gesture of tenderness. "Oh, Will, I'm glad you've come. How happy we were—how happy! I forget everything but that." Devine could not speak for a while. Letty said:

"You'll always be near the children, won't you?"

50

"So help me God! I'll give up my life to them."

Then the doctor came, and the Wanderer saw his stricken wife no more.

Devine bore many hardships before he was able to claim his children, and even when he had rigged up a house fit to shelter them he was vigorously opposed by old Billiter. But he got his own way, and Letty's children joined their father.

And now I must speak of a strange thing. The room which the Wanderer occupies is bare of every comfort. When we sit together we rest our glasses on the mantelpiece (for there is no table), and our feet are on the boards. But one night Devine said, "Come up and see my pets in bed." The young people were disposed in two absolutely comfortable rooms. Everything was neat and clean, and there were signs even of luxury. "How is this? Squalor below, comfort here," I thought. A little girl who was awake said, "Kiss me, papa, dear." Her nightgown was white and pretty. All the clothes that lay around were good. "Now, see the children's room," said my seedy host. "They live *there*." And, behold! a perfectly comfortable place, fitted up with strong, good furniture.

When we went down, the Wanderer helped himself from my flask. Then, with majesty, he observed, "You marvel to see me so shabby? Sir, you must know that I wear my clothes till they are falling to pieces. I deny myself everything but the booze, and I never start on that till I've handed my daughter—bless her!—the best part of the money. I made a promise to a saint, sir. I couldn't drop the liquor. It's my master, so I fight as long as I can and get better as soon as possible after it's over. I'm wrong to give way and spend money on it. I can't help myself. But I give all but my drink-money to them. Sir, I am content to meet the scoffs of respectability; I think only of my children in my sober moments. On the racecourse I'm a gambler, I'm a blackleg (if you believe all you hear); but when the horses are passing the post and all the people are mad, I am quite quiet. I pray sir, to win; but I only pray because my children's faces are before me. Yes, sir, take away the drink and give me a chance of honest work and I might nearly be a good man."

The fellow's face grew almost youthful as he spouted, and I thought, "That little girl upstairs is very young. Her father is not an old man after all." Old he looks—battered, scared, frail; but he has a young heart. What a compound! The more I meditate, the more I am convinced that we shall have to invent a new morality. The standards whereby we judge men are far too rigid. Who shall say that Devine is bad? He is a victim to the disease of alcoholism, and his disease brings with it fits of selfishness. But there is another Devine—the real man—who is neither diseased nor selfish; and both are labelled as disreputable. When next I see poor Billy on the floor after his yelling fit I shall think of him in a friendly way. More than ever I am convinced by his fate that all the high-flying legislation, all the preaching of morality, all pulpit abstractions count for nothing. The best men must try by strenuous individual exertions to combat the subtle curse which has converted the good, generous Billy Devine into a mean débauché. I am out of it. I smoke with Billy, I clink glasses with Billy, I laugh at Billy's declamations, and I am often muddled when I leave Billy in the morning. He illustrates sordidly a chapter of England's history. I wish he didn't.

THE ROBBERY.

I was robbed last night, and it served me right for being a fool. A seedy, down-looking man hangs about The Chèquers all day, and he never does any work except stick up the pins in the skittle alley. He has a sly, secret look, and I fancy he is one of the stupid class of criminals. We often talk together, but there is not much to be got out of him; he usually keeps his eye on someone else's pewter, and he is catholic in his taste for drinks. Of late he has been accompanied by three other persons—a stout, slatternly woman, whom he named as his wife; a rather pretty, snub-nosed girl, who dresses in tawdry prints; and a red-faced, thick-set, dark fellow, who grins perpetually and shows a nice set of teeth. The elder man confidentially informed me that the stout young man was his son-in-law.

We had been a long time acquainted before I learned anything definite about these four. The girl usually arrives about half-past ten; she spends money freely, and the four always take home a huge can of beer. Some while ago the young man—Blackey he is nicknamed—went out, and I followed him quietly. He had been affable with me all the evening, and went so far as to offer me a drink. It struck me that he was indirectly trying to pump me, for he said, "You don't talk like none of us. I reckon you've been on the road." Moreover, when we met he had saluted me thus, "Sarishan Pala. Kushto Bak," and this salutation happens to be Rommany. As we pursued our talk, he inquired, "You rakker Rommanis?" (You speak the gipsy tongue?) and I answered, "Avo." I could see that he wanted to establish some bond of communication between us, and that was why I followed him. As I quietly came up behind him he said, "That's tacho like my dad. I dicked a bar and a pash-crooner." (That's as true as

53

can be. I saw a sovereign and a half-crown.) He was not comfortable when he saw me, and I knew I had been a fool to let him know that I spoke Rommany. However, I passed on as if I had not heard a word. The fellow had no doubt been told that I was a tramp, and he put a feeler to find out whether I knew the language of the road. Next day we met very early. I had stayed out all night with some poachers, and I was in The Chequers by half-past seven in the morning. Master Blackey was there also, and we exchanged greetings. He was blotchy and his eyes seemed heavy; moreover, he was without a drink, and I correctly guessed that he had no money. My evil genius prompted me to ask for brandy-and-soda, which was the last thing I should have done, and Blackey said, "Us blokes can't go for sixpenny drinks. Let me 'ave a drappie levinor." The gipsy word for ale was quietly dropped in, and I ordered the right stuff as if nothing unusual had been said. Then it flashed on me. "This beauty has heard of me from the Suffolk gipsies; he knows that I carry money sometimes, and he wants to find out if I am really the laulo Rye." (The Surrey Roms call me the Boro Rye; the Suffolk Roms call me laulo Rye.)

For a good while after this the times seemed to be rather bad for the four companions. Several times I saw Blackey mutter savagely when the girl came in, and it was easy to see that he was not a full-blood gipsy, or he would never have threatened to strike her in a public bar. Then it happened that I heard a yell one night as I was stealing around the by-streets after most of the drunken people had gone home. A man's voice growled harshly—it was like the snarl of a wild beast,—"Three nights you done no good. Blarst yer slobberin'! you ain't got no more savvey than a blank blank cow. I'd put a new head on yer for tuppence."

A woman answered, "You've struck me, you swine; and if I've got a black eye I'll quod you, sure as I'm yere. Ain't I lushed you, and fed you, and found your clobber long enough?"

"Garn, you farthin' face! Shet your neck."

"All very fine, Mister Blackey, but how would you like a smack in the bloomin' eye? I done the best as I knew for you, and there ain't a bloke round as has a judy wot'll go where I goes and hand over the wongur."

"Never mind, I was waxy when I done it. Maybe we'll 'ave some luck to morrow'."

I was hidden all this time, and I kept very quiet until the pair moved away. Over my last pipe I had many meditations, and formed my own conclusions about Master Blackey.

There are, as I have said, thousands of fellows who have never done any work, and never mean to do any; they are born in various grades of life; the public-house is their temple; they live well and lie warm, and you can see a fine set of them in the full flush of their hoggish jollity at any suburban race meeting. Blackey was a fair specimen of his tribe; they are often pleasant and plausible in a certain way, and it is really a pity that they cannot be forcibly drafted into the army, for they are always men of fine physique. They are vermin, if you like, but how admirably we protect them, and how convenient are the houses of call which we provide for them.

I went warily to work with Blackey, but I was resolved all the same to see him in his home. It happens that even Blackey's household has a hanger-on, who also happens to be a parasite of mine. He is a lanky, weedy lad, with a foxy face. His dark, oblique-set eyes, his high cheek-bones, his sharp chin, are vulpine to the last degree, and, as he slouches along with his shoulders rucked up and his knees bent, he looks like the Representative Thief. He is called Patsey, and I frequently spare him a copper; but his chief patron is Blackey, who often hands him the dregs of a pot of beer.

Yesterday morning Patsey waylaid me, but I waved him off. At night he caught me going in at the back gate of The Chequers; his hand trembled as he clutched my arm, and he said with chattering teeth, "Give me a dollar, and I'll tell you somethin'."

"Tell me the something first, and then we'll see about the dollar."

"Don't you go near Blackey's place tonight. They're a goin' to ast you if they kin. Blackey's found out as you've got respectable relations as wouldn't like to see your name in the papers, and he's goin' to 'ave a new lay on. 'Taint no bloomin' error neither. The gal—Tilley, don't-cherknow—she'll say, 'I'll walk home with you a bit,' when Blackey's out. He meets you, and he says, 'Wot 'cher doin' 'long o' my wife? Didn't I trust you at home? I'll expose you.' *She ain't no more his wife than I am*, so you look out."

"That's worth a dollar, Patsey. Now sneak you into the stables, and don't come near me all night."

I was quite at ease, and became convivial with Blackey and his worthy father-in-law. The only thing that worried me was the knowledge that I had one note in my watch-pocket besides my loose spending money. Still I felt sure of dodging the gang, and I tried to appear innocent as possible while the artless Blackey offered me liquor after liquor; and he remarked at about ten, "My missus orfen says to me, 'Why don't you fetch him home?' she says. If he brings a bottle we'll find our lot, and he'll be just as jolly as he is at Billy Devine's. What say to come down tonight?"

"All right, only not too late."

At twelve we departed, and I was taken to a row of low cottages, which, however, were fairly solid and neat. At first we sat in a kitchen, and I was accommodated with a tub for a seat. Our light came from the fire and a dull lamp, which only made a reddened twilight in the air. The fat woman watched me like a cat, and I fancied that her mouth was like that of a carnivorous beast. The sly old man looked on the ground, but his stealthy eye—like the eye of a cunning magpie—glittered sometimes as he turned it on me. Blackey was most cordial, and soon proposed a song. He obliged first, and warbled some ghastly affair which aimed at being nautical in sentiment. The chorus contained some observations like "Hilley-hiley-Hilley-ho," and it also gave us the information that gentleman named Jack would shortly come home from the sea. The thing was a silly Cockney travesty of a sailor's song, but we were all pleased with it, and it led the way nicely to the girl's ditty, which stated that somebody was going sailing, sailing, over the bounding main (sailors always mention the sea as the bounding main), and by easy steps we got to the fat woman's "Banks of Hallan Worrrtter." We were a jovial company: four of us were wondering how they could rob the fifth, and that fifth resolved, quite early in this sèance, to use his knuckle-duster promptly, and to prevent either of the male warblers from getting behind him, at any risk. About three o'clock the junior lady placed herself on my knee, and her husband approvingly described her as a bloomin' baggage. I did not like the special perfume which my friend employed for her hair, and I also disliked the evidences which went to prove that the bath was not her favourite luxury; but we did not fall out, and, after a spell of sprightly song, we all indulged in a dance of the most spirited description. Drink was plentiful, and, as I saw I was being plied very freely, I pretended to be eager for more. This modified the strategy of my friends, for they were reasonably anxious to secure a skinful, and they feared lest my powers might prove to be abnormal. Four watching like wild beasts! One waiting, and calculating chances! The sullen, grey-eyed old man had taken on the aspect of a ferret; the fat woman was like that awful wretch who meets the pale girl in Hogarth's "Marriage à la Mode;" the bastard gipsy smiled in "leary" fashion, as if he were coming up for the second round of a fight, and knew that he had it all own way. I pumped up jokes, and my snub-nosed charmer pretended to laugh. Ah! what a laugh.

This was the position when Blackey declared that he must go. "Got to shunt, old man? You squat still, now, and git through that there lotion. I got to go to market, and we ain't no bloomin' moke. I'm on on my stand ten o'clock—no later—and that wants doin'. The missus'll fetch me some corrfee, and, hear you, put a nip o' that booze in. It warms yer liver up. By-by. Mind you stay, now, and no faint hearts. Mother, up with your heavy wet, and try suthin' short. I'm off!"

With an ostentatious farewell, the excellent Blackey stumped off, and the four remaining revellers became staid.

"'Ard times," said the ferret-faced man; "but we've 'ad *one* good night out on it anyways."

"How do you make your living, may I ask, if that's a fair question, mate?" This question was addressed by *me* to the sly man, and he was embarrassed.

"Livin'! 'Taint no livin'. It's lingerin'. Leastways it would be if it wasn't for my gell, Tilley, there. 'Er and 'er 'usban' gives us a 'and; an' if you've got a bit about you you might 'elp us put our copper to rights. Got a thick 'un? I'll pay it back, s'elp me Gord, if the missus can start laundryin' agin'."

I saw that this meant "Show us which pocket you keep your money in," so I shamelessly said, "I'll put that square in the morning, governor." Then some silly small-talk—petty as children's babble, low as the cackle of the bar—went on, and I found myself somehow left alone with the snub-nosed young person. She was evidently in some trouble, and I was the more interested about her in that I chanced to look at a side window, and found the fat, carnivorous woman and the down-looking man surveying us with interest, under the impression that they were invisible.

Now, I have never cared for talking to girls of her class, for I do not like them. All talk about soiled doves and the rest is mere nauseous twaddle, arising from ignorance. The creatures take to their rackety life because they like it, and, though I have met some good and kind members of their class, I have observed that the majority are rapacious, cruel, and devoid of every human sentiment that does not hinge on hunger or vanity. You may treat a man as an equal in spite of his vices, and do no harm, but to treat a woman as an equal *because* of her vices is worse than folly. This silly creature proposed to brush my hair. I had encouraged her to familiarity, so I did not object to the toilet process, but I did most strongly object to sniffing at a bottle which she said would "freshen me up amazing." She withdrew the cork, and memories of the college laboratory struck at my brain with sudden violence on the instant. The unforgettable odour of ethyllic chloride caught at my nerves, and I politely rose.

"Pardon me, I must go. It will be daylight in half an hour," I said, for I saw that merry Miss Tilley had been ready to supplement Blackey's device by a second trick.

"I'll come with you a little way. You're dotty a bit."

I reached the fresh air and quietly said, "No, you mustn't. The men are going to factory up by the Fawcett-road, and every second man we meet will know us."

Miss Tilley muttered something, but she preserved her smile and only said, "I tell my husband as you took care of us."

As I stole through the heavy fog I thought, "Now, what business had I there? If my mother had seen that wretched servant girl brushing my hair the old lady would have died—I, the child of many prayers, the hope of a house, and stumping home on a foggy morning after sitting among the scum of earth all night. I mean to be a philosopher, but what a beastly, silly school to cultivate political philosophy in! What do I know more than I knew before?—that one vulgar girl maintains three vulgar criminals, and that all the four will come whining to the workhouse when the game is played out and they can rob no one else. They are creatures whose vices and idleness and general villany are engendered amid drink. They are the foul fungi that fatten on the walls of the public-house; that is all. And I have given them more drink only to see them plan a robbery. Seventy thousand of them in London? Yes. But supposing a few thousands of *us*, instead of being indifferent, instead of 'exploring' in my harum-scarum way, go to work and try to give these creatures a chance of living human lives? What then? Would Blackey or the girl or the wicked old folk have gone to the bar and eaten away their morality with alcohol if they had not been driven out by the stinking dulness of that kitchen? I don't know. I only know that when this spell is over I shall have some corrections to address to the people who stick up institutes, and organise charitable funds. I can offer myself as the horrid example, if they like, and that should impress them."

Then my musings were checked, for I had to cross a wooden bridge over the odious stream that poisoned Teddy, and the fog was like flying gruel. Carefully I picked my way over the bridge, and aimed for the dark, narrow lane that led towards my abode. I remember thinking, "What a place this would be if we were troubled with footpads!" Then came a pause. Now you know how sound travels in a fog? I saw two posts standing shadowily before me; then the posts appeared to fade away, or to be closed up in the brown haze; then I distinctly heard a whisper, "He ain't got her with him. You come after me." I was stooping, and peering to find out who whispered. Wrench! I grasped at my neck. Crack! A sound like the clanking of chains rattled in my head; a flash of many coloured flame shot before my eyes; a hundred memories came vividly to me, and I thought I was a boy again, and then I remember no more, until some voice said, "Feelin' better?"

I was a little sick, and my head was bleeding, but otherwise I had suffered no harm, and I could walk. It was as though I had received a knock-down blow in a fight, and that does not hurt one for long. But how lucky that the water was out of the mill stream! I had been pitched into about six inches of water, and a policeman who heard the splash jumped over some rails, and cut across a private paddock in time to save me from being smothered in the mud. It is now midnight; I have a man with me, and I am not quite so vigorous as I could wish, but my head is clear, and tomorrow there will only be the criss-cross mass of sticking-plaster to tell that I have been felled and robbed. I shall try to pay Mr. Blackey out. Meantime the police and public should remember that many men in London pick up a living by arranging humorous little midnight interviews like that which I went through. Only the professionals work on the Thames Embankment, and the "bashed" man, instead of going into six inches of mud, never is heard of again till his carcass is brought before the coroner.

ONE OF OUR ENTERTAINMENTS.

We have lately had "sport" brought to our very doors, and a pretty crew offered themselves for my study. In the diseased life of the city many odious human types are developed, but none are so horrible as those that crop up at sporting gatherings of various sorts. I have never doubted the existence of an impartial, beneficent Ruling Power save when I have been among the scum of the sporting meetings. At those times I often failed to understand why a good God could permit beings to remain on earth whose very presence seems at once to insult the pure sky and the memory of Christ. If you go away for a few weeks and live among simple fishermen or hinds you become proud of your countrymen. On wild nights, when the black waves galloped down on our vessel and crashed along our decks, I have felt my heart glow as I watched the cool seamen picking up their ropes and working deftly on amid the roaring darkness. The fishers are sober, splendid men, who face death with never a tremor, and toil on usefully day after day. Come away from their broad, sane simplicity and courage, and look upon the infamous hounds who are bred in the congested regions—you are sickened and depressed.

I notice that the sporting gang talk only of betting, thieving, whoremongering, or fighting. With regard to the latter pursuit, their views are distinctly peculiar. A sudden, murderous rush in a crowded bar, a quick, sly blow, and a run away—that is their notion of a manly combat. In the days of the Tipton Slasher two Englishmen would fight fairly like bulldogs for an hour at a stretch; no man thought of crowing about a chance bit of bloodshed, or even a knock-down, for it was understood that the combatants should fight on until one could not rise;

then they shook hands, and were friends. But the brutes whom I now see are transformed Englishmen; they know that a fair upstanding contest would not suit them, and their object is to land one cunning blow, then to make as much noise as possible so as to attract attention. It is cruelly funny to see a gaping blackguard, who has chanced to give someone a black eye or a swollen nose, swaggering round like an absurd bantam, and posing as a sort of athletic champion. The gang are nearly always full of stories about their miserable scrambling fights, and anyone might fancy he had got among a regular corps of paladins to hear them vapour. One marvellously vile betting person haunts me like a disease. The animal has a head like a sea-urchin, his lips are blubbery, his tongue is too big for his mouth, and his face is like one that you see in a nightmare. The ugly head is stuck on a body which resembles a sack of rancid engine grease. This beauty is a fairly representative specimen of our bold sportsmen. He is a deft swindler, and I have gazed with blank innocence while he rooked some courageous simpleton at tossing. The fat, rancid man can do almost as he chooses with a handful of coins, and the marvellous celerity with which sovereigns or halfpence glide between his podgy fingers is quite fascinating. On the subjects of adultery and fighting this object is great, and his foul voice resounds greasily amid our meetings of brave sportsmen. He is accompanied by a choice selection of gay spirits, and I take leave to say that the popular conception of hell is quite barren and poor compared with the howling reality that we can show on any day when a little "sport" is to the fore. I am tolerant enough, but I do seriously think that there are certain assemblies which might be wiped out with advantage to the world by means of a judicious distribution of prussic acid.

Among my weaknesses must be numbered a strong fancy for keeping dogs of various breeds. When you come to understand the animals you can make friends of them, and I have lived in perfect contentment for months at a stretch with no company but my terriers. A favourite terrier often goes about with me now, and the other day Mr. Landlord said, with insinuating softness, "We must have your pup entered for our coursing meeting." It mattered little to me one way or the other, so I paid the entrance fee, and forgot all about the engagement. Coursing with terriers is a very popular "sport" in the south country, and the squat little white-and-tan dogs are bred with all the care that used to be bestowed on fine strains of greyhounds. I cannot quite see where the sport comes in, but many men of all classes enjoy it, and I have no mind to find fault with a remarkable institution which has taken fast root in England. All coursing is cruel; a hare suffers the extremity of agony from the moment when she hears the thud of the dogs' feet until she is whirled round and shaken in those deadly jaws. I lay once amongst straggling furze while a hare and two greyhounds rushed down towards me. Puss had travelled a mile on a Suffolk marsh, and she was failing fast. As she neared me the greyhounds made a violent effort, and the foremost one struck just opposite my hiding-place. Never in my life have I seen such a picture of agony; the poor little beast wrung herself sharp round with a scream—such a scream!—and the dog only succeeded in snatching a mouthful of fur. He lay down, and the hare hobbled into the cover. I could see her tremble. The same sort of torture is inflicted when hares are bundled out of an enclosure with the rapidity and precision of machinery. There is a wild flurry, an agony of one minute or so, and all is over.

The mystery of man's cruelty is inexplicable to me; I feel the mad blood pouring hard when the quarry rushes away, and the snaky dogs dash from the slips; no thought of pity enters my mind for a time because the mysterious wild-man instinct possesses me, and so I suppose that the primeval hunter is ignobly represented by the people who go to see rabbit coursing. We have been refining and refining, and educating the people for a good while; yet our popular sports seems to grow more and more cruel. We do not bait bulls now, but we worry hares and rabbits by the gross, we massacre scores of pretty pigeons—sweet little birds that are slaughtered without a sign of fair play.

Decidedly the Briton likes the savour of blood to mingle with his pleasures. A thousand of ordinary men will gather at Gateshead or Hanley and howl with delight when two wiry whippets worry a stupefied rabbit. They are decent fellows in their way, and they generally have a rigid idea of fairness; but they fail to see the unfairness of hooking a rabbit out of a sack and setting him to run for his life in an enclosure from which he cannot possibly escape. Pastimes that do not involve the death of something or the wagering of money are accounted tame. It is one of the riddles that make me wish I could not think at all. I give it up, for I am only a Loafer, and the dark problems of existence are beyond me.

Perhaps they are beyond Mr. Herbert Spencer.

Our ragged regiment met in a wide, quiet field. Nearly all my costers were about, and they cried "Wayo!" with cordiality. Half the company on the field could not muster threepence in the world; many of them were probably hungry; many were far gone in drink; but all were eager for "sport." We shall have some talk presently about the bitter ennui of the poor man's life. The existence of that deadly ennui never was brought before me so vividly as it was when I saw that queer multitude, forgetting hunger, cold, poverty, pain—and forgetting because they were about to see some rabbits worried!

On a low stand stood a broad pair of scales and an immense hamper. The stand was watched by a red-faced merryandrew, who gibbered and yelled in a vigorous manner. A funny reprobate is that old person. Every hour of his life is given over to the search for excitement; he is never dull; he has a cheery word for all whom he meets; he will drink, fight, and even make love, with all the ardour of youth. When there is nothing more exciting to do, he will drive a trotter for twenty miles at break-neck pace. When he dies, his life's work may be easily summed up:—He drank so many quarts of ale; he killed so many pigeons and rabbits. Nothing more.

My terrier made a ferocious dash at the big hamper, and I knew that our victims were there. Presently the dogs began to arrive, and I was amazed and amused to see some of the little brutes. They could no more catch a rabbit on fair ground than they could pull down a locomotive; but the long railway journey, the strange field, and the clamorous mob render poor Bunny almost helpless, and he gives up his life only too easily. The best of the terriers were beautiful wretches with iron muscles and a general air of courageous wickedness. Their bloodthirstiness was appalling; they knew exactly what was to happen, and their sharp yells of rapture made a din that set my head swimming. Each of them writhed and strained at the collar, and I caught myself wondering what the poor rabbits thought (can they think?) as they heard the wild chiming of that demon pack. In the country, when a dog gives tongue Bunny sits up and twirls his ears uneasily; then, even if the bark is heard from afar off, the little brown beast darts underground. Alas! there is no friendly burrow in this bleak field, and there is no chance of escape; for the merry roughs will soon finish any rabbit that shows the dogs a clean pair of heels.

The ceremony of weighing was completed in a dignified way, and the first brace of dogs went to the slipper. One was a sprightly smooth terrier, with a long, richly-marked head; he was quivering with anticipation, and his demeanour offered a marked contrast to that of the dour, composed brute pitted against him. The rabbit was lifted out of the hamper by one of those greasy nondescript males, who are always to be seen when pigeon shooting or coursing is going on. The greasy being held the rabbit by the ears, and put it temptingly near the dogs. The sprightly terrier went clean demented; the sullen one stood with thoughtful earnestness waiting for a chance to catch the start. When the rabbit was put down it cowered low and seemed trying to shrink into the ground; its ears were pressed hard back, its head was pressed closely to the grass, and it was huddled in an ecstasy of terror. Of course that is quite usual, but we practical sportsmen cannot waste time over the sentimental terrors of a rabbit. The greasy man uttered a howl, and Bunny started up, ran in a circle, and then set off for the fence. I was struck by the animal's mode of running. For hours I have watched them feeding, at early morning or sundown, and I have noticed that as they shifted from place to place they moved with a slow kind of hop, gathering their hind legs under them at each stride. When Bunny is on his own ground he is one of the fastest of four-footed things. He lays himself down to the ground, and travels at such a terrific pace for about forty yards that he looks like a mere streak on the ground. I never yet saw a terrier that could turn a rabbit unless Bunny was imprudent enough to wander more than one hundred yards from home. But this wretched brute in our field was moving at the pace proper to feeding time, and, judging by its deliberate sluggishness, it seemed to be inviting death. When the short pitter-patter of the terriers' feet sounded on the grass, Bunny made a clumsy attempt to quicken his pace; the leading dog plunged at him, and by a convulsive effort the rabbit managed to swirl round and get clear. Then the second dog shot in; then came one or two quick, nervous jerks from side to side; then the beaten creature faltered, and was instantly seized and swung into the air. A good wild rabbit would have been half-way across the next field, but that unhappy invalid had no chance.

The other courses were of much the same character, for the rabbit, being used to run on a beaten path, has not the resource and dexterity of the hare. One strong specimen distanced the pair of tiny weeds that were set after him, but the pack of roughs were whooping at the border of the field, and the doomed rabbit was soon clutched and pocketed.

The betting was furious; a few hard-faced, well-dressed men did their wagering quietly and to heavy amounts, but the mob yelled and squabbled and cursed after their usual manner, and they were all ready to drink when we returned. This is a fair description of rabbit coursing, and I leave influential persons to decide as to whether or no it is a useful or improving form of entertainment. I have my doubts, but must be severely impartial. I will say this, however, that if any one of us had spent the afternoon over a good novel, or something of that kind, he would have been taken out of himself, and, when he rose, his mind would have been filled with quiet and gracious thoughts. Our gang were suffering from a form of the lust for blood; they were thirsty, and they were possessed by that species of excitement which makes a man ready to turn savage on any, or no, provocation.

The bar was like the place of damned souls until eight o'clock: everybody roared at the top of his voice; nobody listened to anybody else, and everybody drank more or less feverishly. We had a supper to celebrate the destruction of the rabbits, and afterwards the truculent gentlemen, who had bellowed so vigorously in the field, sang sentimental songs about "Mother, dear mother," "Stay with me, my darling, stay," or patriotic songs referring to an article of drapery known as "The Flag of Old Hengland."

For half-an-hour our intricate choruses resounded as we went in groups deviously homeward, and a few members of our sporting flock dotted the paths at wide intervals.

That kind of thing goes on all over the country in the winter time. It is not for me to preach, but I must say that it seems to be a barren kind of game. Can any man of the crowd think kindly or clearly about any subject under the sun? I fancy not. My own real idea of the character of the various mobs that see the rabbits die is such that I could not venture to frame it in words. The sport is so mean, so trivial, so purposeless, that I should go a long way to avoid seeing it now that I know the subject well.

And that unspeakably atrocious pettiness forms the only relaxation of a very considerable number of Englishmen. If any member of a corporation were to propose that a great hall should be opened free, and that good music should be provided at the expense of the community, I suppose there would be a deal of grumbling; but I am ready to prove that expenses indirectly caused by our mad "sporting" would more than cover the cost of a rational spell of pleasure.

Honourable gentlemen and worthy aldermen are allowing a great mass of people to remain in a brutalised condition; those people only derive pleasure from the suffering of dumb creatures.

How will it be if the callous crew take it into their heads at some or other to show restiveness? Will they deal gently or thoughtfully with those against whom their enmity is turned? Certainly their education by no means tends to foster gentleness and thoughtfulness. If I were a statesman instead of a Loafer, I reckon I should try might and main to humanise those neglected folk—and they *are* neglected—before they teach some of us a terrific lesson.

I see that one "Walter Besant" has some capital notions concerning the subject which I have ventured to touch on. If he were a rough—as I am during much of my time—he would be able to talk more to the purpose. Still, I deliberately say that that novelist, who is often treated as a moony creature, is a very wise and practical statesman, and he has used his opportunities well. If powerful people do not very soon pay heed to his message, they will have reason for regret.

The worst of it is that one is constantly being forced to wonder whether culture is of any use. For instance, on the day after the coursing, I fell in with a smart lad who loafs about race meetings, and who sometimes visits the landlord's parlour at the Chequers. He has been a year out of Oxford, and he is rather a pretty hand at classics; yet he tries to look and talk like a jockey, and his mother has to keep him because he won't do any work. A shrewd little thing he is, and this is how we talked:—

"Shall I drive you over to the meeting tomorrow?"

"If you like."

"We can do a bit together if you'll dress yourself decently. Barrett says there's a new hunter coming out. It could win the Cesarewitch with 8st. 4lb., but they mean keeping his hunter's certificate. Put a bit on."

"Wait till we see."

"Lord! If I could get the mater to part—only a pony—I'd buy a satchel and start bookmaking in the half-crown ring myself. It's Tom Tiddler's ground if you've got a nut on you."

"Queer work for a 'Varsity man?"

"Deed sight better than bear-leading, or going usher in a school. Fun! Change! Fly about! What more do you want?"

"Do you like to hear the ring curse? Dick and Alf often make me goose-skinned."

"What matter, so you cop the ready?"

"Do you read now?"

"Not such a Juggins. I think my Oxford time was all wasted. Of course, I liked to hear Jowett palaver, and it was quiet and nice enough; but give me life. Bet all day; dinner at the Rainbow, Pav., or Trocadéro, and Globe to finish up. That's life!"

If anyone had chances this youth had them, and now his ambition is to bet half-crowns with the riddlings of Creation. This universe is getting to be a little too much for me. Come down, pipe; I shall go in the Chequers parlour tonight, and play the settled citizen.

MERRY JERRY AND HIS FRIENDS.

I never saw such a cheerful face as Jerry's. Master Blackey can smile and smile; he can smile on me even now, though I know almost to a certainty that it was he who left that discoloured ring round my throat not long ago. But Blackey can scowl also, whereas Jerry never ceases to look benignant and jolly. He is a fine young fellow is Jerry, six feet high, straight as a lance, ruddy, clear-skinned, and with the bluest, brightest eye you can see. When he walks he is upright and stately as the best of Guardsmen, without any military stiffness; when he spars he is active as a leopard, and his mode of landing with his left is at once terrible and artistic. Sometimes he drinks a little too much, and then his sweet smile becomes fatuous, but he never is unpleasant. The girls from the factory admire him sincerely; they call him Merry Jerry, and he accepts their homage with serenity. He never takes the trouble to show any deference towards his admirers; their amorous glances and giggling are inevitable tributes to his fascinations, and he takes it all as a matter of course. Like Blackey and the Ramper, Jerry never does any work, and he is supposed to have private means. His speech is quite correct, and even elegant, and although he does not converse on exalted topics, he is a singularly pleasant companion in his way. Most of his talk is about horse-racing, and he never reads anything but the sporting papers. In that taste he resembles most of those who go to The Chequers. The wrangling, the cursing, the whispered confidences that make up the nightly volume of noise nearly all have reference to racing subjects. The raggedest wretch at the bar puts on horsey airs when any great race is to be decided; he may not know a horse from a mule, but he invariably volunteers his opinion, and if he can raise a shilling he backs his fancy. Polite gentlemen in Parliament and elsewhere do not appear to know that there are something like one million British adults whose chief interest in life (apart from their necessary daily work) is centred on racing. I think I know almost every town in England, and I never yet in all my wanderings settled at an inn without finding that betting of some sort or other formed the main subject of conversation. Hundreds of times—literally hundreds—I have known whole evenings devoted to discussing the odds. The gamblers were usually men who did not care to see horses gallop; they chatted about names, and that satisfied them. A clerk, a mechanic, a tradesman, a traveller, a publican asks his friend what he has done over such and such a race, just as he asks after the friend's health. It is taken for granted that everybody bets, and really intelligent fellows will stare at you in astonishment if you say that you are not interested in the result of a race. If I chose to make a book—only dealing in small sums—I could contrive to win a fair amount every week by merely "betting to figures." The bookmaker does not need to visit a racecourse; he is required to work out a sort of algebraical problem on each race, and, by exercising a little shrewdness, he may leave himself a small balance on every event. Small sums in silver are always forthcoming to almost any extent, and a clever man who has no more than £100 capital to start with may pitch his tent almost anywhere, and make sure of getting plenty of custom. People speak of the Italians as gamblers, but in Italy gambling is not nearly so prevalent as in England. In Manchester alone one sporting journal has a morning and evening edition, and there are daily papers in most of the large Yorkshire towns. In the North-country I have often watched the workmen during the breakfast half-hour, and found that they did not care a rush for anything in the paper save the sporting news. In London two great journals are published daily, and twice a week each of them issues a double number. Every line of these papers is devoted to sport, and each of them is a rich estate to the proprietor.

The mania for betting grows more acute every day, the number of wealthy bookmakers increases, and the national demoralisation has reached a depth which would seem inconceivable to anyone who has not lived with all sorts and conditions of men. A racing man is apt to become incapable of concentrating his mind on anything except his one pursuit. Hundreds of thoughtful and cultured people race a little and bet a little by way of relaxation; but these take no harm. It is the ignorant, ill-balanced folk, without higher interests, who suffer.

Well-meaning persons spend money on respectable institutes for working men, but the men do not care for staid, dull proceedings after their work is over; they want excitement. A moderately heavy bet supplies them with a topic for conversation; it gives them all the keen pleasures of anticipation as the day of the race draws near, and when they open the paper to see the final result they are thrilled just as a gambler is thrilled when he throws the dice. No wonder that the mild and moral places of recreation are left empty; no wonder that the public-houses are well filled. If I were asked to name two things which interest the English nation to the supreme degree, I should say—first, Sport; second, Drink. If the strongest Ministry that ever took office attempted to make betting a criminal offence, they would be turned out in a month. Betting is now not a casual amusement, but a serious national pursuit. The perfect honesty with which payments are made by agents is amazing. A man who bets on commission for others may have £100,000 to lay out on a race; every farthing is accounted for, and dishonesty among the higher grades of the betting brotherhood is practically unknown. It is this rigid observance of the point of honour that tempts people like our gang in The Chequers bar to risk their shillings; they know that if they make a right guess their payment is safe. The statesman who called the turf "a vast instrument of national demoralization" was quite right, and if he could have lived to take a tour round the country in this year of grace he would have seen the flower of his nation given over to mean frivolity.

Jerry has tutored me in racing matters. He has not a thought that is not derived from the columns of the sporting prints, and his life is passed mainly in searching like a staunch terrier for "certainties." When he is disposed to be communicative, he soon gathers quite an audience in The Chequers, and should he drop a phrase like "George Robinson said to me, 'I've made my own book for Highflyer,'" or "Charley White, the Duke's Motto, wouldn't lay Mountebank any more," the awe-stricken costers stare. Here is a man, a regular toff, and no error—a man who knows such Ringmen as Robinson and White—and yet he will speak to ordinary coves without exhibiting the least pride!

Jerry has taken me round to the best haunts where gallant sportsmen assemble, and for some mysterious reason, his escort has secured for me the most flattering deference. Queer holes he knows by the score. I thought I had seen most things; but I find I am a babe compared with Jerry. He once said to me, "Would you like to see a couple of lads set-to? Real good 'uns." I had seen a great number of encounters; but my two pounds handed over to Jerry procured me a sight of a battle which was the most desperate affair I ever witnessed. But for the close, oppressive atmosphere of the room where the fight took place, the whole business would have been interesting. The spectators were well dressed and well behaved, the boxers were beautiful athletes, and there was nothing repulsive about the swift exchange of lightning blows until the baking heat began to tell on the men; then it was disagreeable to see two gallant fellows panting and labouring for breath. We often hear that boxing is discredited. Rubbish! Ask Jerry about that, and you will learn that any company of men who care to subscribe £25 may see a combat wherein science, courage, and endurance are all displayed lavishly.

Jerry was much interested in dog fighting, which latter pleasing pastime is enjoyed quite freely in London to an extent that would amaze the gentlemen who rejoice over the decline of brutality in Britain.

The competitive instinct which once found vent in fighting and conquest now works on other lines. The Englishman must be engaged in a contest, or he is unhappy, and, since he cannot now compete sword to sword with his fellow-creatures, he fights purse to purse instead. All these things I knew in a vague way, but Jerry has made my knowledge definite and secure.

As for the man himself, I soon found that his "private means" were taken in various ways from other people's pockets. During a chat, he said, "You know you're not what you pretend to be. You hang about there, and you bet, but you never bet enough to make anything at it. You must have the coins, for I've seen you spend a quid in two hours in the skittle-alley. But you don't seem to best anybody. What *is* your game? You may as well tell me."

"I amuse myself in my own way, and I don't care to let the school know much about me."

"Well, my game's very simple. Only a juggins or a horse ever works, and I don't intend to do any. It's just as easy to be idle as not. You take the fellows in town that make their living after dark, and you always see them having good times. There's some red-hot ones up—you know where—in Piccadilly; they never get about till close on dinner time, but they make up for lost time when they *are* about. I should like to work with you. If you were to come out a bit flash like me, why, with your looks and your talk and that *educated* kind of way you've got, you might coin money."

"But you wouldn't care to work the Embankment and run the risk of the cat, as those Piccadilly chaps do?"

"No fear. But you could do better than that. When you're boozed you're not in it—you lose your head; but when you're right you make fellows wonder what you are. Sink me! A flat would pal on to you in half an hour if you coaxed him, as you can do it."

Jerry is an amusing philosopher, who could only have been developed in the rottenness of a decadence. Fancy an able-bodied, attractive fellow living with ease from day to day without doing a stroke of honest labour. He keeps clear of the police; he gratifies every want, yet he has the intellect of a flash potman and the manners of a valet. The tribe swarm in this city, and I reckon that they will teach us something when the overturn comes. They are strong and cunning predatory animals, who will direct weak and stupid predatory animals, and when the entire predatory tribe smash the flimsy bonds with which society holds them in check for the present, then stand by for ugly times.

I hate the revolver, but I am glad that I took to carrying one in time. Jerry and I grew so intimate, and I saw so much of his inner mind, that I judged it better to make no midnight excursions in his company without being ready for accidents. He is most humorous when he has wine in him, and his humour is a shade too grim for my taste.

We came home lately in a cab, after seeing a pretty little light-weight from Birmingham receive a severe dressing at the hands of a pocket Hercules from Bethnal Green. Jerry was in wild spirits, and his usual charming smile had broadened into a grin. Nothing would suit him but that I should go to his rooms.

"My aunt keeps house for me, and she's sure to be up, and my sister's there as well."

The notion of Jerry's dwelling calmly with his aunt and his sister was very touching, and my curiosity was roused. The aunt turned out to be a placid woman with a low voice; the sister was too florid and loud for my fancy. We played at whist, and in the intervals between the games we tested Jerry's wine. He has a singularly good selection. The florid nymph was reserved and coy at first, but as the wine mounted she rather astonished me by her choice of expletives. The merry one had become business-like, and that sweet smile was gone. As I looked at him I gradually understood that I had once more made a fool of myself, and I vowed that if I got out safely I would go to The Chequers no more. Over-confidence is a bad fault in a prize-fighter: it is worse than that in the case of a man who wishes to hold his own among London sharps. Blackey had the best of me, and now I was in for a much worse business. Jerry the Amiable drank ostentatiously, and he was evidently priming himself; the sister waxed effusive, and the aunt took care that the points were steadily increased. In the early morning the Amiable suggested that I should stay, but I would not have slept under the same roof with him for gold. He then ordered his relatives off to bed, and they slunk away rather like dogs than ladies. Jerry was a masterful man. When all was quiet I rose to take my hat, whereupon Jerry remarked, "You're not going that way, are you?"

"Must go home before it's too light."

"You'll have another drink?"

"No."

"But you will!"

The Amiable was really extremely exacting.

"Thanks. Good morning."

Jerry locked the door, and put his back to it. Then he softly said, "You've come home and taken my liquor; you flirt with my sister, and you're going away without leaving so much as a bit of gold. I'm not such a fool as Blackey. I know your aunt. I can send a newspaper to her address, and cook *your* goose. Suppose I make a row. I can do that, and we'll both be taken up for brawling outside a house of ill-fame. It won't matter to me; I'm used to it. But you'll be spoofed. Now, share up with an old pal, and I'll keep dark."

I had contrived to edge away from him, and I had time to produce the detestable firearm in a leisurely way.

"You're very kind, Jerry, my lad. I'll stay at this side of the room, and I shan't fire so long as you keep still. If you try to strike or put your hand in your pocket I shall pull on you; If you care to raise your arms over your head and move to the right-hand corner of the room I'll go quietly."

Jerry reckoned up all the chances and finally edged away from the door.

"Hands up, Jerry."

He obeyed, and I escaped into the street. Jerry is a coward at bottom, or he might have known that I dare not fire.

He met me the very next day, and he wore the usual free, gay smile. He held out his hand and flashed his teeth: "Forget that nonsense last night, old pal. When the booze is in—you know the rest. I was only having a lark. What'll you have? We shall be glad to see you round again."

But Mr. Landlord had dropped a word to me only half an hour before. Said Mr. Landlord, in answer to a little careless pumping, "Oh, Jerry? Well, it ain't no business of mine, but if it wasn't for the girls he'd have mighty few flash top-coats, nor beefsteaks neither for that matter."

Alas! Jerry, the smiling, delightful youth, is one of those odious pests who hang about in sporting company, and who are contemned and shunned by respectable racing men. Said a grave turfite to me last week, "Call *those* sportsmen! I'd—I'd—" but he could not invent a doom horrid enough for them, so he changed the subject with a mighty snort.

There is no knowing what gentlemen like Jerry will do. To call them scoundrels is to flatter them: they are brigands, and the knifing, lounging rascals of Sicily and Calabria are mere children in villany compared with their English imitators. Places like The Chequers are the hunting-grounds of creatures like Jerry, and the bait of drink draws the victims thither ready to be sacrificed. A month ago four of Jerry's gang most heartlessly robbed a publican who had sold his business. He had the purchase-money in his pocket, and the fellows drugged him. He ought to have known better, seeing how often he had watched the brigands operating on other people; but as he lost £700, and as his assailants are still at large with their shares of the spoil, we must not reproach him or add to his misery.

I picked out Jerry for portraiture because he is a fairly typical specimen of a bad—a very bad—set. When the history of our decline and fall comes to be Written by some Australian Gibbon, the historian may choose the British bully and turfite to set alongside of the awful creatures who preyed on the rich fools of wicked old Rome.

THE GENTLEMAN, THE DOCTOR, AND DICKY.

We have had enough of the roughs for a time, and I want now to deal with a few of the wrecks that I see—wrecks that started their voyage with every promise of prosperity. Let no young fellow who reads what follows fancy that he is safe. He may be laborious; an unguarded moment after a spell of severe work may see him take the first step to ruin. He may be brilliant: his brilliancy of intellect, by causing him to be courted, may lead him into idleness, and idleness is the bed whereon parasitic vices flourish rankly. Take warning.

I was invited to go for a drive, but I had letters to write, and said so. A quiet old man who was sitting in the darkest corner of the bar spoke to me softly, "If your letters are merely about ordinary business, you may dictate them to me here, and I will transcribe them and send them off." I replied that I could do them as quickly myself. The old man smiled. "You do not send letters in shorthand. I can take a hundred and forty words a minute, and you can do your correspondence and go away." The oddity of the proposal attracted me. I agreed to dictate. The old man took out his notebook, and in ten minutes the work was done. We came back in an hour, and by that time each letter was transcribed in a beautiful, delicate longhand. I handed the scribe a shilling, and he was satisfied. The Gentleman, as we called him, writes letters for anyone who can spare him a glass of liquor or a few coppers; but I had never tested his skill before. There was no one in the bar, so I sat down beside the old man, and we talked.

"You seem wonderfully clever at shorthand. I am surprised that you haven't permanent work."

"It would do me little good. I can go on for a long time, but when my fit comes on me I am not long in losing any job. They won't have me, friend—they won't have me."

"You've been well employed, then, in your time?"

"No one better. If I had command of myself, I might have done as well in my way as my brother has in his. I could beat him once, and I was quite as industrious as he was; but, when I came to the crossroads, I took the wrong turning, and here I am."

"May I ask how your brother succeeded? I mean—what is he?"

"He is Chief Justice—."

I found that this was quite true; indeed, the Gentleman was one of the most veracious men I have known.

"Does your brother know how you are faring?"

"He did know, but I never trouble him. He was a good fellow to me, and I have never worried him for years. I prefer to be dead to the world. I have haunted this place, as you know, for six months; tomorrow I may make a change, and live in another sty."

"But surely you could get chance work that would keep you in decent clothes and food."

"I do get many chance jobs; but if the money amounts to much I am apt to be taken up as drunk and incapable."

The sweet, quiet smile which accompanied this amazing statement was touching. The old man had a fine, thoughtful face, and only a slight bulbousness of the nose gave sign of his failing. Properly dressed, he would have looked like a professor, or doctor, or something of that kind. As it was, his air of good breeding and culture quite accounted for the name the people gave him. I should have found it impossible to imagine him in a police-cell had I not been a midnight wanderer for long.

"How did you come to learn shorthand?"

"My father was a solicitor in large practice, and I found I could assist him with the confidential correspondence, so I took lessons in White's system for a year. My father said I was his right hand. Ah! He gave me ten pounds and two days' holiday at Brighton when I took down his first letter."

"Have you been a solicitor?"

"No. I had an idea of putting my name down at one of the Inns, but I went wrong before anything came of the affair."

"You say you have had good employment. But how did you contrive to separate from your father?"

"Oh! I wore out his patience. I was so successful that I thought it safe to toast my success. We were in a south-country town—Sussex, you know—and I began by hanging about the hotel in the market-place. Then I played cards at night with some of the fast hands, and was useless and shaky in the mornings. Then I began to have periodical fits of drunkenness; then I became quite untrustworthy, and last of all I robbed my father during a bad fit, and we parted."

"And then?"

"I picked up odd jobs for newspapers, or sponged on my brother. At last I was sent to the House as reporter, and did very well until one night when Palmerston was expected to make an important speech. My turn came, and I was blind and helpless. Since then I have been in place after place, but the end was always the same, and I have learned that I am a hopeless, worthless wretch."

"But couldn't your brother, for his own credit's sake, keep you in his house and put you under treatment?"

"My good friend, I should die under it. I revel in degradation. I luxuriate in self-contempt. My time is short, and I want to pass it away speedily. This life suits me, for I seldom have my senses, and there is only the early morning to dread. I think then—think, think, think. Until I can scrape together my first liquor I see ugly things. I should be in my own town with my grandchildren round me. I might have been on the Bench, like my brother, and all men would have respected me as they do him. Sons and daughters would have gathered round me when I came to my last hour. I gave it all up in order to sluice my throat with brandy and gin. That is the way I think in the morning. Then I take a glass, or beg one, as I shall from you presently, and then I forget. Once I went out to commit suicide, and took three whiskies to string my nerve up. In two minutes I was laughing at a Punch and Judy show. If you'll kindly order a quartern of gin in a pint glass for me, I'll fill it up and be quite content all the evening. No one ill-uses me. I'm a soft, harmless, disreputable old ne'er-do-well. That is all."

We drank, and then the Gentleman said, "You come here a good deal too much. Your hand was not quite right yesterday morning. Usually you keep right, and I really don't know how far you are touched. If I had your youth and your appearance, I think I should save myself in time by a bold step. Join the temperance people and work publicly; then you are committed, and you can't step back."

"But you don't think that I am likely to go to the dogs? I loaf around here because I have no ambition, and my life was settled for me; but I have command over myself."

"You *had* command over yourself, you mean. I think you are in great danger—very great indeed. My good friend, there are *no* exceptions. Meet me tonight, or say tomorrow, as I am to be drunk tonight; go to the beer-house at the end of my street, and I'll show you something."

Just then the Ramper came up and hailed the Gentleman. "Here you old swine! Are you sober enough to scratch off a letter?"

"I'm all right."

"Well, then, write to the usual, and tell him to put me on half-a-quid Sunshine, and half-a-quid Dartmoor a shop—s.p. both."

Thus our conversation was stopped, and the brother of a judge earned twopence by writing a letter for a racecourse thief.

Next night I went to a very shady public-house, and the Gentleman led me into a dirty room, where a little old man was sitting alone. The man was crooked, wizened, weak, and his bare toes stuck out of both shoes; his half-rotten frock coat gaped at the breast and showed that he had no shirt on; his hat must have been picked up from a dustheap, for it was filthy, and broken in three or four places.

"For mercy's sake, give me a mouthful of something!" said this object, turning the face of a mummy towards me. His dim eyes were rheumy, and his chin trembled. An awful sight!

In a flash I remembered him, and cried, "What, Doctor!"

He said, "I don't know you; my memory's gone. Send for twopenn'orth or a penn'orth of beer. Pray do."

My young friends, that man who begged for a pennyworth of muddy ale was first of all a brilliant soldier, then a brilliant lawyer, then a brilliant historian. His doctor's degree—he was Doctor of Laws—was gained by fair hard work. Think of that, and then look at my picture of the sodden, filthy scarecrow! Yes; that man began my education, and had I only gone straight on I should not be loafing about The Chequers. You ask how he could have anything to do with my education? Well, long ago I was a little bookworm, living in a lonely country house, and I had the run of some good shelves. I was only nine years old, but a huge history in two volumes attracted me most. I read and read that book until I could repeat whole pages easily, and even now I can go off at score if you give me a start.

The Scarecrow wrote that history!

Years afterwards I was fighting my way in London, and had charge of a journal which made a name in its day. Sometimes I had to deal with a message from a Minister of State, sometimes with a petition from a starving penny-a-liner. One day a little man was shown into my room, which room was instantly scented with whisky. He was well introduced, and I said, "Are you the Doctor—who wrote the 'History of—'?"

"I am, sir, and proud I shall be to write for you."

"What can you do?"

"Here's a specimen."

The MS. was a bundle of bills from a public-house, and the blank side was utilised. The Doctor never wasted money on paper when he could avoid it. The stuff was feeble, involved, useless. My face must have fallen, for the piteous Scarecrow said, "I have not your approval."

"We cannot use this."

Bending forward and clasping his hands, he said, "Could you not give me two shillings for it? There are two columns good. A shilling a column; surely that can't hurt you."

"I'll give you two shillings, and you can come back again if you are needy, but the MS. is of no use to us."

He took the money, and returned again and again for more. I found that he used to put fourpence in one pocket to meet the expense of his lodging-house bed, and he bought ten two-pennyworths of gin with the rest of the money. He always asked for two shillings, and always got it. I was not responsible for his mode of spending it.

And now the Doctor had turned up in the region of The Chequers. He was piteously, doggishly thankful for his drink, and he cried as he bleated out his prayers for my good health. Men cry readily when they come to be in the Doctor's condition. I asked him to take some soup. "I'm no great eater," he said; "but I'd like just one more with you—only one."

"Where do you lodge, Doctor?"

"To tell you the truth, I'm forced to put up with a berth in the old fowl-house at the bottom of the garden here. They let me stay there, but 'tis cold—cold."

"Do you work at all now?"

"Sometimes. But there is little doing—very little."

"How did you come to cease practising at the Bar, Doctor?"

"How do I come to be here? 'Tis the old thing—the old thing—and has been all along."

This poor wretch could not be allowed to go about half-naked, so I let the potman run out and get him a slop suit. (The Doctor sold the clothes next day for half-a-crown, and was speechless when I went to see him.) A hopeless, helpless wretch was the Doctor—the most hopeless I ever knew. He entered the army, early in life, and for a time he was petted and courted in Dublin society. The man was handsome, accomplished, and brilliantly clever, and success seemed to follow him. He sold out of the army and went to the Bar, where he succeeded during many years. No one could have lived a happier, fuller, or more fruitful life than he did before he slid into loose habits. His only pastime was the pursuit of literature, and he finished his big history of a certain great war while he was in full practice at the Chancery Bar. Power seemed to reside in him; fortune poured gifts on him; and he lost all. In an incredibly short space of time he drank away his practice, his reputation, his hopes of high honour, his last penny.

Thus it was that my historian came to beg of me for that muddy penn'orth.

I may as well finish the Doctor's story. If I were writing fiction the tale would be scouted as improbable, yet I am going to state plain facts. A firm of lawyers hunted up the Doctor, and informed him that he had succeeded to the sum of £30,000. There was no mistake about the matter; the long years of vile degradation, the rags, the squalor, the scorn, of men were all to disappear. The solicitors dressed the Doctor properly and advanced him money; he set off for Ireland to make some necessary arrangements, and he solemnly swore that he would become a total abstainer. At Swindon he chose to break his journey, took to drinking, and kept on for many hours. It was long since he had had such a chance of unlimited drink, and he greedily seized it. When he went to bed he took a bottle with him, and in the morning he was dead. Suffocated by alcohol, they said. He had no living soul related to him, and I believe his money went to the Crown.

I have written this last fragment on separate sheets, and my journal is interleaved for the first time.

The Gentleman and I became very friendly. I never tried to keep him from drinking: it was useless. When he was sober his company was pleasant, and I was very sorry when he mysteriously migrated, and many of our crew missed his help badly.

Some time after the Gentleman's flight, I was in a common lodging-house in Holborn, and in the kitchen I met a delightful vagabond of a Frenchman with whom I had a long talk. He happened to say, "One of our old friends died last week. He was a good man, and very well bred. Figure it to yourself, he was brother of one of your judges!" Then I knew that the Gentleman had gone. I wish I could have seen him again. As I look back at the old leaves of my journal I seem to see that sweet, patient smile which he wore as he told the story of his fall. There are some things almost too sad to bear thinking about. This is one.

* * * * *

Our friend Dicky had a bad misfortune lately. I should say that Dicky is an oldish man, who drifted into this ugly quarter some time ago, and took his place in the parlour, which is a room that I now prefer to the bar. I was holding a friendly discussion with a butcher when a strident voice said, "You are absolutely and irredeemably ignorant of the rudiments of your subject." I started. Where had I heard that voice before? The man was clad in an old shooting-jacket; his trousers were out at the knee, and his linen was very dirty; yet there was a something about him—a kind of distinction—which was impressive. After launching his expression of contempt at us, he buried his face in his pot and took a mighty drink. Slowly my memory aided me, and under that knobby, pustuled skin I traced the features of Dicky Nash, the most dreaded political journalist of my time. Often I had heard that voice roaring blasphemies with a vigour that no other man could equal; often had I seen that sturdy form extended beside the editorial chair, while the fumes in the office told tales as to the cause of the fall. And now here was Dicky—ragged, dirty, and evidently down on his luck. I soon made friends with him by owning his superior authority, and he kindly took a quart of ale at my expense. This was a man who used to earn £2,000 a year after he resigned his University fellowship. He was the friend and adviser of statesmen; he might have ended as a Cabinet Minister, for no man ever succeeded in gauging the extent of his miraculous ability; he seemed to be the most powerful, as well as the most dreaded man in England. Woe is me! We had to carry him up to bed; and he stayed on until he spent a three-guinea cheque, which Mr. Landlord cashed for him.

I knew no good would come of his Fleet-street games, though he used to laugh things off himself. He would come in about seven in the evening, and seat himself at his table. Then he would hiccup, "Can't write politics; no good. Give us a nice light subject."

"Try an article on the country at this season of the year."

"Good. I can't hold the damned pen. You sit down, I'll dictate: In this refulgent season, when the barred clouds bloom the soft dying day, it is pleasant to wander by the purple hedgerows where the stars of the (What damned flower is it that twinkles now? What do you say? Ragged Robin? Not poetic enough. Clematis? That'll do. Damn it, ride on!)—the stars of the clematis modestly twinkle, and the trailing—(What the h—is it that trails? Honeysuckle? Good. Weigh in!)—trailing honeysuckle flings down that rich scent that falls like sweet music on the nerves.'"

And so on. He managed in this way to turn out the regulation column of flummery, but I knew it could not last. And now he had come to be a sot and an outcast. Worse has befallen him. He screwed up his nerve to write an article in the old style, and I helped him by acting as amanuensis. He violently attacked an editor who had persistently befriended him; then he wrote a London Letter for that editor's paper; then he sent the violent attack away in the envelope intended for the letter. There was a terrible quarrel.

So far did the Gentleman, the Doctor, and Dicky come down. I may say that Dicky, the companion of statesmen, the pride of his university, died of cold and hunger in a cellar in the Borough. Oh, young man, boast not of thy strength!

POACHERS AND NIGHTBIRDS.

The Chequers stands in a very nasty place, yet we are within easy distance of a park which swarms with game. This game is preserved for the amusement of a royal duke, who is kind enough to draw about twelve thousand a year from the admiring taxpayer. He has not rendered any very brilliant service to his adopted country, unless we reckon his nearly causing the loss of the battle of Alma as a national benefit. He wept piteously during the battle of Inkerman when the Guards got into a warm corner, but, although he is pleasingly merciful towards Russians, he is most courageous in his assaults on pheasants and rabbits, and the country provides him with the finest sporting ground in England. I should not like to say how many men make money by poaching in the park, but we have a regular school of them at The Chequers, and they seem to pick up a fair amount of drink money. The temptation is great. Every one of these poaching fellows has the hunter's instinct strongly developed, and neither fines nor gaol can frighten them. The keepers catch one after another, but the work goes on all the same. You cannot stop men from poaching, and there is an end of the matter. You may shout yourself hoarse in trying to bring a greyhound to heel after he sights a hare; but the dog *cannot* obey you, for he is an automaton. The human predatory animal has his share of reason, but he also is automatic to some degree, and he will hunt in spite of all perils and all punishments when he sights his prey. One comic old rascal whom I know well has been caught thirty times and imprisoned eight times. While he is in gaol he always occupies himself in composing songs in praise of poaching, and on the evening of his release he is invariably called on to furnish the company in the tap-room with his new composition. He cannot read or write, but he learns his songs by heart, and I have taken down a large number of them from his own lips. The things are much like Jemmy Catnach's stuff, so far as rhyme and rhythm are concerned, but they are interesting on account of the sly exultation that runs through them.

In one poem the lawless bard gives an account of a day's life in gaol, and his coarse phrases make you almost feel the cold and hunger. Here are some scraps from this descriptive work:—

"Till seven we walk around the yard,
There is a man all to you guard.
If you put your hand out so,
Untoe the guv'nor you must go;
Eight o'clock is our breakfast hour,
Those wittles they do soon devour;
Oh! dear me, how they eat and stuff,
Lave off with less than half enough.
Nine o'clock you mount the mill,
That you mayn't cramp from settin' still.
If that be ever so against your will,
You must mount on the traädin' mill.
There is a turnkey that you'll find
He is a raskill most unkind.
To rob poor prisoners he is that man,
To chaäte poor prisoners where he can.
At eleven o'clock we march upstairs
To hear the parson read the prayers.
Then we are locked into a pen—
It's almost like a lion's den.
There's iron bars big round as your thigh,
To make you of a prison shy.
At twelve o'clock the turnkey come;

The locks and bolts sound like a drum.
If you be ever so full of game,
The traädin' mill it will you tame.
At one you mount the mill again,
That is labour all in vain
If that be ever so wrong or right,
You must traäde till six at night.
Thursdays we have a jubal fraä
Wi' bread and cheese for all the day.
I'll tell you raälly, without consate,
For a hungry pig 'tis a charmin' bait.
At six you're locked into your cell,
There until the mornin' dwell;
There's a bed o' straw all to lay on,
There's Hobson's choice, there's that or none."

That is a bleak picture; but the old man winds up by bidding all his mates "go it again, my merry boys, and never mind if they you taäke." He told me that on several occasions he was out ferreting, or with his lurcher, on the next night after coming out of prison. Can you keep such a fellow out of a well-stocked park? He likes the money that he gets for game, but what he likes far better is the wild pleasure of seeing the deadly dogs wind on the trail of the doomed quarry; he likes the danger, the strategy, the gambling chances.

One night I got this old man to drive me about for some hours. He is a smart hand with horses, and when I said, "Can you manage without lamps in this dark?"—he answered, "I could find my way for twenty miles round here if you tie my eyes up. There's nary gate that my nets hasn't been under; there's hardly a field that I haven't been chased on." As our trotter swung on, I found that the poacher associated almost every gate and outhouse and copse with some wild story. For example, we passed a clump of farm-buildings, and the poacher said; "I had a queer job in there. Three of us had had a good night—a dozen hares—and we got half-a-crown apiece for them, so we drank all day, and came out on the game again at night. We put down a master lot o' wires about eleven, and then we takes a bottle o' rum and goes to lie down on a load of hay. Well, we all takes too much, and sleeps on and on. When I wakes, Lord, we was covered with snow, and a marcy we was alive. We dursn't go for our wires in the daylight, and there we has to stand and see a keeper go and take out three hares, one after another. It was a fortnight before I had a chance of picking up the wires again, and we was about perished." Cold, wet, and all other inconveniences are nothing to the poacher.

Presently my man chuckled grimly. "Had a near shave over there where you see them ar' trees. I had my old dorg out one night, and two commarades along with me. We did werra well at that gate we just passed, so we tries another field. Do you think that there owd dorg 'ud go in? Not he. There never was such a one for 'cuteness. We was all in our poachin' clothes, faces blacked, women's nightcaps on, and shirts on over our coats. Well, the light come in the sky, and I separates from my mates, for I sees the owd dorg put up a hare and coorse her. I follows him, and he gits up for first turn; then puss begins to turn very quick to throw the dorg out before she made her last run to cover. He was on the scut, the old rip—catch him leave her—and I gits excited, and, like a fool, I chevies him on. In a minute I sees a man running at me, and off I goes for the gate. Now, I could run any man round here from 300 yards up to a mile; but I knew I must be took at the gate, unless I could stop the keeper. I had a big stick with me—about six foot long it was—and did sometimes to beat fuzz with; so I takes the stick by one end. He come up very sharp, and I made up my mind to let him gain on me. As soon as I *feels* him on me, I swings round, and the stick got him on the side of the head. He went flat down, and I got on to the road. I picked up my mates, and we washes our faces in a pond; then we leaves our clothes with one of the school, and walks off to the pub. Half an hour after, in comes the keeper and says, 'See what some of you blackguards has done for me?'

I stands him a drink and says how sorry, and we parted. Ah! Years after that I was at a harvest supper with that keeper, and we talks of that affair. I says, 'I'll tell you now, I was the man as knocked you over,' and he says, 'Shake hands, Tom. It was the cleanest thing I ever saw done.'

"Do you really like the game, then?"

"Like it! I'd die at it. If it wasn't for my crippled foot I'd be out every night now."

Old Tom, the much-imprisoned man, never goes out with a gang now, but his influence is potent. He is the romantic poacher, and many a man has been set on by him. Observe that the best of these night thieves are on perfectly friendly terms with the keepers. If they are taken, they resign themselves to fate, and bear no ill-will. It is a game, and if the keeper makes a good move he is admired—and forgiven.

Six regular poachers come daily to The Chequers, but there are many others hanging around who are merely amateurs. One queer customer with whom I have stayed out many nights is the despair of the keepers. His resource is inexhaustible, and his courage is almost admirable. Let me say—with a blush if you like—that I am a skilful poacher, and my generalship has met with approval from gentlemen who have often seen the inside of Her Majesty's prisons. Alas!

One day I was much taken with the appearance of a beautiful fawn bitch, which lay on the seat in the room which is used by the most shady men in the district. Her owner was a tall, thin man, with sly grey eyes, set very near together, and a lean, resolute face. Doggy men are freemasons, and I soon opened the conversation by speaking of the pretty fawn. She pricked her ears, and to my amazement, they stood up like those of a rabbit. Such a weird, out-of-the-way head I never saw, though the dog looked a nice, well-trained greyhound when she had her ears laid back.

I said, "Why, she's a lurcher."

"She ain't all greyhound; but the best man as ever I knew always said there never was a prick-eared one a bad 'un."

"Is she for sale?"

"There ain't enough money to buy her."

"She's so very good?"

"Never was one like her!"

I found out, when we became fast friends, that the man's statement was quite correct. The dog's intelligence was supernatural. For the benefit of innocents who do not know what poaching is like, I will give an idea of this one dog's depredations. The owner—the Consumptive, I call him, as his night work has damaged his lungs—grew very friendly one day, and confidential. He winked and remarked, "Now, how many do you think I've had this month?"

"How many what?"

"You know. Rabbits. Guess."

I tried, and failed. The Consumptive whispered, "Well, I keeps count, just the same as a shopkeeper, and as true as I'm a living man I've taken two hundred and fifty out of that park, and averaged tenpence for 'em."

"With the one bitch?"

"No. I've got a pup from her—such a pup. The old 'un's taught the baby, and I swear I'll never let that pup come out in daylight. They work together, and nothing can get away."

This astounding statement was true to the letter. The dogs were like imps for cunning; they would hide skilfully at the very sound of a strange footstep, and they would retrieve for miles if necessary. I may say that I have seen them at work, and I earnestly wish that Frank Buckland could have been there.

The Consumptive is a dissolute, drunken fellow, whose life is certainly not noble. Fancy being maintained in idleness by a couple of dogs! But the park is there, and the man cannot help stealing. I have seen his puppy, and I wish the royal duke could see her. She is a cross between lurcher and greyhound; her cunning head resembles that of a terrier, and her long, slim limbs are hard as steel. Her precious owner spends his days in tippling; he never reads, and, I fancy, never thinks; he goes forth at dusk, and his faithful dogs proceed to work for his livelihood.

The Consumptive is, as I have said, a man of great resource; but he has for once been within a hair's breadth of disaster. When he walks across the park at dusk, he likes to take his wife with him, and on such occasions he looks like a quiet workman out for a stroll with the missus. He sometimes puts his arm round the lady's waist, and the couple look so very loving and tender. It would never do to take the raking, great deerhound; but the innocent little fawn dog naturally follows her master, and looks, oh! so demure.

The lady wears a wide loose cloak, which comes to her feet, for you must know that the mists rise very coldly from the hollows. Then these two sentimentalists wend their way to a secluded quarter of the vast park, and presently the faithful fawn mysteriously disappears. She moves slyly among the bracken, and her exquisite scent serves to guide her unerringly as she works up wind. Presently she steadies herself, takes aim, and rushes! The rabbit only has time to turn once or twice before the savage jaws close on him, and then the fawn makes her way carefully towards Darby and Joan. She takes advantage of every shadow; she never thinks of rashly crossing open ground, and Darby has only got to stamp twice to make her lie down. She sneaks up, and, horror! she gives the rabbit to Joan. Now under that cloak there is a useful little apparatus. A strong strap is fastened under Joan's armpits and over her breasts. This strap has on it a dozen strong hooks. Joan slits away the tendons of the rabbit's hind legs from the bone, hangs the game on one of the hooks, and the lovers wend their way peacefully, while the family provider glides off on another murderous errand. When four or five hooks are occupied, the lady walks homeward with the demure dog, Darby goes and drinks at The Chequers till about eleven, and then the mouse-coloured deerhound is taken out to do her share.

The fond couple were sitting on a bench under a tree, for Joan had fairly tired under the weight of no less than nine rabbits which were slung on her belt. The lurcher stole up, and quietly laid a rabbit down at Joan's feet; then a soft-spoken man came from behind the tree, and observed—

"I am a policeman in plain clothes, and you must go with me to the keeper's cottage."

But Darby, the wily one, rose to the occasion. The dog is trained to repudiate his acquaintance at a word, and when he said, "That's not my dog; get off, you brute!" the accomplished lurcher picked up the rabbit and vanished like lightning. Nevertheless the policeman led off Darby, and Joan followed. The keeper was out, but the policeman searched the Consumptive and found nothing.

The keeper said to me—even me, "My wife tells me they brought up a man the other night, but he had no game on him. He had a woman with him that fairly made the missus tremble. She was like a bloomin' giant out of a show." I smiled, for the Consumptive had told me the whole tale. "My 'art was in my mouth," he remarked, and I do not wonder. Considering that Joan was padded with the carcases of *nine* rabbits under that enormous cloak, it was quite natural for her bulk to seem abnormal. Ah! if that intelligent policeman had probed the mysteries that underlay the cloak! I am glad he did not, for the Consumptive is a most entertaining beast of prey.

Another of our poaching men was obliged to borrow from me the money for his dog licences, and in gratitude he allowed me to see his brace of greyhounds work at midnight. People think that greyhounds cannot hunt by scent, but this man has a tiny black and a large brindle that work like basset-hounds. They are partners, and they have apparently a great contempt for the rules of coursing. One waits at the bottom of a field, while his partner quarters the ground with the arrowy fleetness of a swallow. When a hare is put up by the beating dog she goes straight to her doom.

It seems marvellous that such lawless desperadoes should be hanging about London; but there they are, and they will have successors so long as there is a head of game on the ground. The men are disreputable loafers;

they care only for drink and the pleasures of idleness. I grant that. My only business is to show what a strange secret life, what a strange secret society, may be studied almost within sight of St. Paul's.

The very best and most daring poacher I know lives within five-and-twenty minutes' journey from Waterloo. You may keep on framing stringent game laws as long as you choose, but you cannot kill an overmastering instinct.

I am not prepared to say, "Abolish the Game Laws;" but I do say that those laws cause wild, worthless fellows to be regarded as heroes. No stigma whatever attaches to a man who has been imprisoned for poaching; he has won his Victoria Cross, and he is admired henceforth. You inflict a punishment which confers honour on the culprit in the eyes of the only persons for whose opinion he cares. Even the better sort of men who haunt our public-houses are glad to meet and talk with the poachers. The punishment gives a man a few weeks of privation and months of adulation. He bears no malice; he simply goes and poaches again. No burglar ever brags of his exploits; the poacher always boasts, and always receives applause.

JIM BILLINGS.

Few people know that large numbers of the splendid seamen who man our North Sea fishing fleets are arrant Cockneys. In the North-country and in Scotland the proud natives are accustomed to regard the Cockney as a being who can only be reckoned as human by very charitable persons. To hear a Scotch fisherman mention a "Kokenee" is an experience which lets you know how far scorn may really be cherished by an earnest man. The Northerners believe that all the manliness and hardiness in the country reside in their persons; but I take leave to dispute that pleasing article of faith, for I have seen hundreds of Londoners who were quite as brave and skilful sailors as any born north of the Tees. The Cockney is a little given to talking, but he is a good man all the same.

In the smacks many lads from the workhouse schools are apprenticed, and some of the smartest skippers in England come originally from Mitcham or Sutton. Jim Billings was a workhouse boy when he first went to sea, and he sometimes ran up to London after his eight weeks' trips were over. When I first cast eyes on Jim I said quite involuntarily, "Bob Travers, by the living man!" The famous coloured boxer is still alive and hearty, and it would be hard to tell the difference between him and Jim Billings were it not that the prize-fighter dresses smartly. Jim doesn't; his huge chest is set off by a coarse white jumper; his corded arms are usually bared nearly to the elbow, and his vast shock of twining curls relieves him generally from the trouble of wearing headgear. On Sundays he sometimes puts on a most comfortless felt hat, but that is merely a chance tribute to social usage, and the ugly excrescence does not disfigure Jim's shaggy head for very long. Billings's father was a mulatto prize-fighter, who perished early from the effects of those raging excesses in which all men of his class indulged when they came out of training. The mulatto was as powerful and game a man as ever stripped in a twenty-four-foot ring; but he ruined his constitution with alcohol, and he left his children penniless. The little bullet-headed Jim was drafted off to the workhouse school, and from thence to a small fishing-smack.

Does anyone ever think nowadays of the horrors that were to be seen among the fleets not so very long ago? It is not a wonder that any of the fishers had a glimmer of human feeling in them when they reached manhood, for no brute beast—not even a cabhorse in an Italian town—was ever treated as an apprentice on a smack was treated. Some of the sea-ruffians carried their cruelty to insane extremes, for the lust of blood seemed to grow upon them. It is a naked truth that there was no law for boys who lived on the high seas until very recent years. One fine, hardy seadog (that is the correct and robust way of talking) used to strip his apprentice, and make him go out to the bowsprit end when the vessel was dipping her stem in winter time. He was such a merry fellow, was this bold seadog, and I could make breezy, "robust" Britons laugh for hours by my narratives of his drolleries. He would not let this poor boy eat a morsel of anything until he had mixed the dish with excrements, and when the lad puked at the food the hardy mariner cut his head open with a belaying-pin or flung him down the hatchway. Sometimes the hardy one and the mate lashed the apprentice up in the fore-rigging, and they had rare sport while he squealed under the sting of the knotted rope's end. On one night the watch on deck saw a figure dart forward and spring on the rail; the contumacious boy had stripped himself, and he was barely saved from throwing his skinny, lacerated carcass into the sea. Shortly after this the youngest apprentice went below, and found the ill-used lad standing on a locker, and gibbering fearfully. The tiny boy said:

"Oh! Jim, Jim, what's come to you?" but James never uttered a rational word more. He was sent to his mother's house at Deptford, and he went to bed with four other children. In the early morning the youngsters noticed that Jim seemed rather stiff, and he had exceedingly good reasons, for he was stone-dead, and doubled up. The coroner's jury thought that death resulted from a stoppage of the intestines. That was very funny indeed, for Jim's shipmates observed that as he was bruised and rope's-ended more and more he lost all power of retaining his food, and everything he swallowed passed from him undigested. Jim succumbed to the wholesome, manly, hardening, maritime discipline of the good old times, and no one was hanged for murdering him.

The mind of the kindly, shoregoing man cannot rightly conceive the monstrosities of cruelty which were perpetrated. Fancy a boy bending over a line and baiting hooks for dear life while the blood from a fearful scalp wound drained his veins till he fainted. The lad came to in four hours; had he died he would have been quietly reported as washed overboard. If you can stand a few hours of talk from an old smacksman you may hear a sombre litany of horror. Those fishers are, physically, the flower of our race, and many of them have the noblest moral qualities. Knowing what I do of the old days, I wonder that the men are any better than desperate savages.

Jim Billings endured the bitterest hardships that could befall an apprentice. For six years he was not allowed to have a bed, for that luxury was generally denied to boys. He secured a piece of old netting, and he used to sleep on that until it became rotten by reason of the salt water which drained from his clothes. On mad winter nights, when the sea came hurling along, and crashed thunderously on the decks, the smack tugged and lunged at her trawl. All round her the dark water boiled and roared, and the blast shrieked through the cordage with hollow tremors. That One who rideth on the wings of the wind lashed the dark sea into aimless fury, and the men on deck clung where they could as the smothering waves broke and seethed in wild eddies over the reeling vessel. At midnight the sleepers below heard the cry, "Haul, O! haul, haul, haul!" and they staggered to their feet in the reeking den of a cabin.

"Does it rain?"

"No, it snows."

That was the fragment of dialogue which passed pretty often. Then the skipper inquired, "Do you want any cinder ashes?" The ashes were spread on the treacherous deck; the bars were fixed in the capstan, and the crew tramped on their chill round. Men often fell asleep at their dreary work, and walked on mechanically; sometimes the struggle lasted for an hour or two, until strong fellows were ready to lie down, and over the straining gang the icy wind roared and the piercing drift flew in vicious streams. When the big beam and the slimy net came to hand the worst of the work began; it often happened that a man who ran against a shipmate was obliged to say, "Who's that?" so dense was the darkness; and yet amid that impenetrable gloom the intricate gear had to be handled with certainty, and when the living avalanche of fish flowed from the great bag, it was necessary to kill, clean, and sort them in the dark. When the toil was over Jim Billings went below with his mates, and their dripping clothes soon covered the cabin floor with slush.

"Surely they changed their clothes?" I fancy I hear some innocent asking that question. Ah! No. The smacksmen have no time for changes of raiment. Jim huddled himself up like the rest: the crew turned in soaking, and woke up steaming, just as the men do even nowadays.

Week in, week out, Jim Billings led that hard life, and he grew up brawny and sound in spite of all his troubles. His frame was a mass of bone and wire, and no man could accurately measure his strength. His mind was left vacant of all good impressions; every purely animal faculty was abnormally developed, and Jim's one notion of relaxation was to get beastly drunk whenever he had the chance. Like too many more of those grand seamen, he came to regard himself as an outcast, for he was cut off from the world during about forty-six weeks of every year, and he thought that no creature on earth cared for him. If he broke a finger or strained a tendon, he must bear his suffering, and labour on until his eight weeks were up; books, newspapers, rational amusements were unknown to him; he lived on amid cursing, fighting, fierce toil, and general bestiality.

Pray, what were Jim's recreations? When he ran up to London he remained violently, aggressively drunk while his money lasted, and at such times he was as dangerous as a Cape buffalo in a rage. With all his weight he was as active as a leopard, and his hitting was as quick as Ned Donnelly's. He enjoyed a fight, but no one who faced him shared his enjoyment long; for he generally settled his man with one rush. He used both hands with awful severity; and in short, he was one of the most fearsome wild beasts ever allowed to remain at large. I have known him to take four men at once, with disastrous results to the four, and, when he had to be conveyed to the police-station (which was rather frequently), fresh men were always brought round to handle him. Speaking personally, I may say that I would rather enter a cage of performing lions than stand up for two rounds with Mr. Billings. He only once was near The Chequers, and I fear I entertained an unholy desire to see some of our peculiar and eloquent pugilists raise his ire. Here was a pretty mass of blackguard manhood for you! Everyone who knew him felt certain that Jim would be sent to penal servitude in the end for killing some antagonist with an unlucky blow; no human power seemed capable of restraining him, and of superhuman powers he only knew one thing—he knew that you use certain words for cursing purposes.

Over the grey desolation of that cruel North Sea no humanising agency ever travelled to soften Jim Billings and his like; but there were many agencies at work to convert the men into brutes.

On calm days there came sinister vessels that sneaked furtively among the fleet. A little black flag flew from the foretopmast stay of these ugly visitors, and that was a sign that tobacco and spirits were on sale aboard. The smacksmen went for tobacco, which is a necessity of life to them; but the clever Dutchmen soon contrived to introduce other wares. Vile aniseed brandy—liquid fire—was sold cheap, and many a man who began the day cool and sober ended it as a raving madman. Mr. Coper, the

Dutch trader, did not care a rush for ready money; ropes, nets, sails were quite as much in his line, and a continual temptation was held out to men who wanted to rob their owners. Jim Billings used to get drunk as often as possible, and he himself told me of one ghastly expedient to which he was reduced when he and his shipmates were parched and craving for more poison. A dead man came past their vessel; they lowered the boat, and proceeded to haul the clothes off the corpse. The putrid flesh came away with the garments, but the drunkards never heeded. They scrubbed the clothes, dried them in the rigging, and coped them away for brandy.

Mr. Coper had other attractions for young and lusty fishermen. There are certain hounds in France, Holland, and even in our own virtuous country, who pick up a living by selling beastly pictures. In the North Sea fleets there are 12,000 powerful fellows who are practically condemned to celibacy, and the human apes who sold the bawdy pictures drove a rare trade among the swarming vessels.

Jim Billings was a capital customer to the Copers, for his animalism ran riot, and he was more like a tremendous automaton than like a man.

So this mighty creature lived his life, drinking, fighting, toiling, blaspheming, and dwelling in rank darkness. He often spoke of "Gord," and his burly childishness tickled me infinitely. I liked Jim; he was such a Man when one compared him with our sharps and noodles; but I never expected to see him fairly distance me in the race towards respectability. I am still a Loafer; Jim is a most estimable member of the gentlest society; and this is how it all came about.

On one grey Sunday morning a pretty smack came creeping through the fleet. Far and near the dark trawlers heaved to the soft swell, and they looked picturesque enough; but the strange vessel was handsomer than any of the fishing-boats, and Jim's curiosity was roused. The new smack was flying a flag at her masthead, but Jim could not read well enough to make out the inscription on the flag. He said, "Who's he?" and his mate answered, "A blank mission ship. Lot o' blokes come round preachin' and prayin'."

"What? To our blank chaps? How is it I've never seen his blank flag afore?"

"Ain't been werry long started. I heerd about 'em at Gorleston. Fat Dan got converted board o' one on 'em."

Just then the smart smack shoved her foresail a-weather and hove-to; then a small boat put out, and a stout grizzled man hailed Jim.

"What cheer, old lad, what cheer? Come and give us a look. Service in an hour's time. Come and have a pot o' tea and a pipe."

I am grieved to say that Mr. Billings remarked, "Let's go aboard the blank, and capsize the whole blank trunk."

Certainly he jumped up the side of the mission ship with very evil intentions. Boat after boat came up and made fast astern of the dandy vessel, and soon the decks were crowded with merry groups. Jim couldn't make it out for the life of him. These fellows had their pipes and cigars going; they were full of fun, and yet Jim could not hear an oath or a lewd word. Gradually he began to feel a little sheepish, but nevertheless he did not relinquish his desire to break up the service. The skipper of the smack invited Jim to go below, and handed him a steaming mug of tea.

"Where's your 'bacca?" said the skipper.

"Left him aboard."

"Never mind. Take half a pound and pay for it tomorrow. We sell the best at a shilling a pound."

Jim gaped. Here was a decidedly practical religious agency. A shilling a pound! Cheaper than the Copers' rubbish. Jim took a few pulls at the strong, black tobacco, and began to reconsider his notion about smashing up the service. He found the religious skipper was as good a fisherman as anyone in the fleet; the talk was free from that horrible cant which scares wild and manly men so easily, and the copper-coloured rowdy almost enjoyed himself.

Presently the lively company filed into the hold, squatted on fish boxes, and proceeded to make themselves comfortable. Two speakers from London were to address the meeting, and Jim gazed very critically on both.

A hymn was sung, and the crash of the hoarse voices sounded weirdly over the moan of the wind. Jim felt something catch at his throat, and yet he was unable to tell what strange new feeling thrilled him. His comrades sang as if their lives depended on their efforts. Jim sat on, half pleased, half sulky, wholly puzzled. Then one of the speakers rose. At first sight the preacher looked like anything but an apostle; his plump, rounded body gave no hint of asceticism, and his merry, pure eye twinkled from the midst of a most rubicund expanse of countenance. He looked like one who had found the world a pleasant place, and Jim gruffly described him as a "jolly old bloke." But the voice of this comfortable, suave-looking missionary by no means matched his appearance. He spoke with a grave and silvery pitch that made his words seem to soar lightly over his audience. His accent was that of the genuine society man, but a delicate touch—a mere suspicion—of Scotch gave the cultured tones a certain odd piquancy. A solemn note of deep passion trembled, as it were, amid the floating music, and every word went home. This jolly, rosy missionary is one of the best of living popular speakers, and his passionate simplicity fairly conquers the very rudest of audiences. The man believes every word he says, and his power of rousing strong emotion has seldom been equalled.

Jim Billings sat and glowered; he understood every simply lucid sentence that the orator uttered, and he was charmed in spite of himself.

"This is the blankest, rummiest blank go ever I was in," muttered the would-be iconoclast.

His visions of a merry riot were all fled, and he was listening with the eagerness of a decorous Sunday-school child.

Speaker Number Two arose, and Jim's bleared eyes were riveted on him. The rough saw before him a pallid, worn man, whose beautiful face seemed drawn by suffering. Long, exquisite artist hands, silky beard, kindly, humorous mouth, marked by stern lines; these were the things that Jim dimly saw. But the dusky blackguard was really daunted and mastered by the preacher's eye. The wonderful eye was like Napoleon's and Mary Stuart's in colour; but the Emperor's lordly look hinted of earthly ambition: the missionary's wide, flashing gaze seemed to be turned on some solemn vision. Twice in my life have I seen such an eye—once in the flesh when I met General Gordon, once in a portrait of Columbus. Poor Jim was fascinated; he was in presence of the hero-martyr who has revolutionised the life of a great population by the sheer force of his own unconquerable will. Jim did not know that the slim man with the royal eye must endure acute agony as he travels from one squalid vessel to another; he did not know that the sublime modern Reformer has overcome colossal difficulties while enduring tortures which would make even brave men pray for death. Jim was in the dark. He only knew that the saintly man talked like a "toff," and said strange things. After a little the "toff" dropped the accent of the Belgravian and began to speak in low, impassioned tones; he told one little story, and Jim found that he must cry or swear. With sorrow I must say that he did the latter, in order to bully the lump out of his bull throat. Then the "toff" broke into a cry of infinite tenderness and pity; he implored the men to come, and some sturdy fellows sobbed; but Jim did not understand where they were wanted to go, and he growled another oath.

After this some of the fishermen spoke, and Jim heard how drunkards, fighting men, and spendthrifts had become peaceable and prosperous citizens.

Puzzles were heaped on the poor man's brain. He could have broken that pale man in halves with one hand; yet the pale man mastered him. He knew some of the burly seamen as old ruffians; yet here they were—talking gently, and boasting about their happiness and prosperity. When the last crashing chorus had been sung, the two swells went round and chatted freely with all comers.

"No—'toffs' never treated me like that afore."

All that day, until the trawl went down, Jim sat growling and brooding. He was inarticulate, and the crowding thoughts that surged in his dim soul were chaotic.

Next day he inquired, "Do you know anything 'bout this yere Jesus as they yarns about?"

"Devil a bit! Get the bloke on the Mission ship to tell you."

"See him and you damned fust!"

Thus spoke the impolite James. But on the ninth day the Mission smack ran into the Blue fleet again, and Jim took a desperate resolution. His boat was astern, so he jumped over the counter and sculled himself straight to the Mission smack.

"Got them gents aboard?"

The skipper was wild with delight at seeing the most notorious ruffian on the coast come voluntarily, and Mr. Billings was soon below in the after cabin. Poor Jim stuttered and haggled while trying to explain what was the matter with him.

"I tell you, guvnor, I've got a something that must come out, or I shall choke straight off. I want to speak, and I can't get no words."

I shall say nothing of the long talk that went on. I know something about it, but the subject is too sacred for a Loafer to touch. I shall only say that Jim Billings got release, as the fishers say, and his wild, infantine outburst made powerful men cry like children.

He is now a very quiet soul, and he neither visits The Chequers nor any other hostelry. There was great fun among the Gorleston men when Jim turned serious, and one merry smacksman actually struck at the quadroon. Jim bit his lip, and said,

"Bill, old lad, I'd have killed you for that a year ago. Shake hands; God bless you!"

Which was rather a plucky thing to do.

Some blathering parsons say that this blessed Mission is teaching men to talk cant and Puritanism. Speaking as a very cynical Loafer, I can only say that if Puritanism turns fishing fleets and fishing towns from being hells on earth into being decent places; if Puritanism heals the sick, comforts the sufferers, carries joy and refinement and culture into places that were once homes of horror, and renders the police force almost a superfluity in two great towns—then I think we can put up with Puritanism.

I know that Jim Billings was a dangerous untamed animal; he is now a jolly, but quiet fellow. I was always rather afraid of him; but now I should not mind sailing in his vessel. The Puritan Mission has civilised him and hundreds on hundreds more, and I wish the parsons had done just half as much.

For my own part, I think that when I am clear of The Chequers I shall go clean away into the North Sea. If on some mad night the last sea heaves us down, and the Loafer is found on some wind-swept beach, that will be as good an end as a burnt-out, careless being can ask. Perhaps Jim Billings, the rough, and I, the broken gentleman, may go triumphantly together. Who knows? I should like to take the last flight with the fighting nigger.

OUR PARLOUR COMPANY.

We have one room where high prices are charged. This place is kept very select indeed, and the vulgar are excluded. I was not received very well at first, and some of the assembly talked at me in a way which was intended to be highly droll; but I never lost temper, and I fairly established my position by dint of good humour. Moreover, I found out who was the most unpopular man in the room, and earned much goodwill by slyly administering the kind of strokes which a fairly educated man can always play off on a dullard. I hate the parlour, and if I were to let out according to my fancy I should use violent language. In that dull, stupid place one learns to appraise the talk about sociality and joviality at its correct value. I am afraid I must utter a heresy. I have heard that George Eliot's chapter about the Raveloe Inn is considered as equal to Shakespeare's work. Now I can only see in it the imaginative writing of a clever woman who tried to dramatise a scene without having any data to guide her. In all my life I never heard a conversation resembling that of the farrier and the rest in the remotest degree. In the first place, one element of public-house talk—the overt or sly indecency—is left out. In an actual public-house parlour the man who can bring in a totally new tale of a dirty nature is the hero of the evening. Then the element of scandal is missing. When men of vulgar mind meet together, you only need to wait a few minutes before you hear someone's character pulled to pieces, and the scandal is usually of the clumsiest sort. Again, it is easy to represent the landlord as a pliable person who agrees with everybody; but the landlord of real life is a person who is treated with deference, and who asserts his position in the most pronounced fashion. If he has a good customer he is courteous and obliging, but he keeps a strict hand on his company, and lets them know who is master. Nearly all the landlords I have known since I became a Loafer have been good fellows. They find it in their interest to be generous, obliging, and friendly; but to represent them as timorous sycophants is absurd. They are ordinary tradesmen; they have a good opinion of themselves, and they hold their own with all classes of men. The women are sometimes insolent, overdressed creatures, who heartily despise their customers; but very often a landlord marries a lady who is as far as possible from being like the hostess of fiction.

The temperance orators destroy their main chance of gaining a success by their senseless attempts to be funny at the expense of the licensed victuallers. Any spouter who chooses to rant about the landlady's gold chain and silk dress can make sure of a laugh, and anyone who talks about "prosperous Mr. Bung" is approved. For the sake of a good cause I beg the abstainers to tell the plain, brutal truth as I do, and refrain from scandalising a decent class of citizens. Why on earth should the landlord be named as a pariah among the virtuous classes? He is a capitalist who is tempted to invest money in a trade which is the mainstay of our revenue; he is hedged in with restrictions, and the faintest slip ruins him for ever. The very nature of his business compels him to be smart, obliging, ostentatiously friendly; yet with all this the Government treat him as if he were by nature a thief, while thousands of earnest but ignorant and foolish people reckon him an enemy of society.

Pray who is forced or solicited to buy the landlord's wares? Your butcher cries "Buy, buy, buy!" your draper sends out bills and sandwichmen; but the publican would be scouted if he went out touting for custom. If a man asks for drink he knows quite well what he is doing, and if he takes too much it is because of some morbid taint or unlucky weakness.

Take away the taint, and strengthen the weakness; but do not pour blackguard and unfair abuse on business men who are in no way answerable for human frailty.

When I hear (as I often do) some flabby boozer whining and ascribing his trouble to the drinkshop, I despise him. Who took him to the drinkshop? Was it not to please himself that he went? Did he care for any other being's gratification but his own when he slipped the alcohol down his throat? Yet he appeals for pity. I reckon that I know England and Scotland as well as most commercial travellers, and I have been compelled to depend for my comfort and well-being on the men whom some of the Alliance folk call pariahs. In all my experience I have come across less than a dozen men whom I should imagine to rank among the shady division. I should be a liar if I said that many public-houses are highly moral and useful institutions; but the abuses are due to the rank faults of human nature, and not to the class of traders who are alternately described as venal sycophants or robbers. Let us be fair. The Devil has enough to bear, and for any harm which we bring to ourselves we should not lay the blame on him or fate.

The whole Raveloe scene is full of typical errors. It is too pretty, too decent, too neat, too humourous. There is very little fun to be got out of public-house humours, because the vanity of the various talkers is offensive, and their stupidity has not the charm of simplicity. If such a man as, say, Mr. Matthew Arnold wanted to test the accuracy of the "Silas Marner" chapter for critical purposes, he would scarcely recover the ordeal of a night spent in a haunt of the hardened toper. If the company happened to be unembarrassed, their ribaldry would sicken the philosopher; their coarse manners would revolt him; their political talk—well, that would probably stupefy him and cause him to flee.

Here are my notes of one specimen conversation, given without any dramatic nonsense or idealisation. My memory can be trusted absolutely, and I have often reported a long interview in such a way that the person interviewed saw nothing to alter.

Bowman guffawed, and his purple face swelled with merriment, for he had been hearing a whispered story told by Bill Preston, an elderly retired tradesman. Bill is a most respectable man whose daughters hold quite a leading position in the society of our district. He is great on church business, and he is the vicar's right-hand man. It is a noble sight to see him on Sundays when he stalks down the aisle, nattily dressed in black, and wearing a devotional air; but in our parlour his sole aim is to tell the queerest stories in the greatest possible number, and his collection—amassed by years of loving industry—is large and various. He cannot hear the simplest speech without trying to extract some bawdy significance from it, and when he has scored a thoroughly indecent success, his clean, rosy, jolly face is lit up by a fascinating smile. Ah! if ladies only heard these sober fathers of families when conversational high jinks are in progress, they would be decidedly enlightened.

When Bowman ended his guffaw he said, with admiration, "You naughty old man! How dare you go for to corrupt my morals?" And Bill received the tribute with modest gratification. Then a loud voice silenced us all, and Joe Pidgeon, our great logician, began to hold forth.

"Wot did old Disraely do? Why, they was all frightened of him. He was a masterpiece, I tell you. What was that there heppigram as he made?—'Inebriated with the hexuberance of his own verbosity.' There's langwidge for you! And he kep' it up, too, he did. He was the brightest diadem in England's crown, he was. But this Gladstone!—wot's he? Show me any trade as he's benefited! Ain't he taken the British Flag to the bloomin' pawnshop? Gord love me, he oughter be 'ung, he did! I tell you he ought to be 'ung. If you was to say to me tomorrow 'Will you 'ang old Gladstone?' I'd 'andle the rope. He's a blank robber and a scoundrel, he is.

"What's this new man, Lord Churchill, goin' to do? He's a red-hot 'un. He does slip into 'em, and no mistake. He's a coming man, I reckon. I never see such a flow of language as that bit where he called old Gommy a superannuated Pharisee. That was up against him, wasn't it?"

An old man spoke. He is feeble, but he is regarded as an authority on literature, politics, and other matters. "There's never been a good day for anybody since the old-fashioned elections was done away with. All the houses was open, fun going on for days, and the candidates was free as free could be. Your vote was worth something then. I remember when Horsley put up against Palmer. A rare man was Palmer! Why, that Palmer drove down with a coach-and-four and postilions, and he kept us all alive for a week. He'd kiss the children in the streets, and he'd set all the taps free in any inn that he went into. It's all purity and that sort of thing now.

"I don't see no good in talking politics. One of the jiggers says one thing, and one of them says another thing. I think the first one's right, then I think the other one's right, and then I think nothing at all. I say, give us something good for trade, and let us have a fair chance of making money. That's my motto.

"And, I say, let's have a law to turn those d—d Germans out of the country. They come over here—the hungry, poverty-stricken brutes—and they take the bread out of Englishmen's mouths, and they talk about education. Education! who cares for education? I never could read a book in my life without falling asleep, and I can give some of the educated ones a start in my small way. Why, I've got a tenant—a literary man—and he has about six pound of meat sent home in a week. There's education for you. I say, out with the Germans!"

Rullock, the cultured man, was hurt when he heard education mentioned lightly. He said, "Excuse *me*, friend Bowler, but I think we must reckonise the claims of edgication. We all know you; we all respect you, and we know you'll cut up well at the finish; but I must disagree with you on that one subject. I'm a edgicated man—I may say that much. My father paid sixty pound a year at boarding-school for me. Sixty—pounds—a—year; so if I'm not edgicated, I should like to know who is. It's a great advantage to you. Look at the position you take when you go into a public room, and talk about any subject that comes up. Suppose you're ignorant; well, there you sit; and what are you? You're nobody. No, I approve of edgication—it improves the mind. It does undoubtedly improve the mind. Look now at this Randolph Churchill that's come to the front. What is it but edgication that brought him forward? I should venture to say he's a learned man, and knows lots of languages and sciences, else how'd he shut up such a wonderful orator as Gladstone? We all know as old Beaky was edgicated. Look at his books. How'd he write a book without it? I began "Cohningsby," and, I tell you, it's grand—sublime. No, friend B., I think you must give in I'm right."

"And I think you're a lot of—fools."

This interruption came from the devout Billy—Billy Preston. That pious man liked to have the talk mainly to himself, and he thought that anything not obscene was tame. By the way, these abrupt and insolent remarks are characteristic of public-house wit. A favourite joke is to ask a friend a serious question. When he fails to answer, then the joker shouts some totally irrelevant and indecent word, and the questioned man is regarded as "sold." I cannot repeat the interlude with which Billy Preston favoured us, but it was very spicy indeed, and referred to some of those sacred secrets which are known to all. For a pillar of the Church, Billy displayed rather amazing tastes and abilities. Then the talk fell into decency after the regulation merriment had greeted Mr. Preston's closing effort.

"How long will you give Jobson to hold out?"

"I don't know. He's into everybody's books all round. I should like to pick up that pony if he does smash."

"I heard Charley Dunn say that Mrs. Jobson was round at old Burdett's asking for time. Jimmy Burdett's got a lot of Jobson's paper, and I shouldn't wonder if he stole a march on the other creditors."

"Well, Jobson's a good sort, but he couldn't last. He's too free with his money. I never wanted his champagne and his suppers, but you had to drop in like the others, and there you are."

A strident voice drowned the scandal, and an admiring group ceased smoking and listened spellbound to a characteristic anecdote. I cannot put in all the expletives, but I may say that the speaker modelled his style on that of the more eloquent betting men whom he knew.

"I says to him, you'll trot me, will you? Why, go on with you, run and see your grandmother, and get her to wipe your nose for you. Strike me, I could sweep the blank chimney with you! You want to get on to me, and you know my cob can't go more than eleven at the outside. I was kiddin' him on, do you see? Then I winks at old Sammy, and he says, very solemn, 'It's absurd for you, sir, to talk of trotting this gentleman. The cob's out of condition, and rough as a badger.' You see I let the cob keep his winter coat, and he was an object and no error. So this bloke was a fly flat, don't you know, and I could see he bit. He says, 'I'd like to have a match with you.' So I tips the office to Sammy, and blanked if he didn't go and knock in a slice of bloomin' flint a little way between the shoe and the near fore foot. I says very timid, 'Well, sir, I don't mind having a try just for a bit of sport, if you'll lay £30 to £20.' He says, 'Done with you,' and we staked. When I sees my pony walking gingerly, I made as if I was took aback. He saw the same thing, and says, 'Pony's wrong.' 'Yes,' says I, 'worse luck.' He says, 'I lay you £50 to £30 I beat you.' I says, 'You have me at a disadvantage, sir, but I'm on,' and I pulls out my three tenners. Then Sammy got the flint out, and we went into the road. I let him go away, and after we'd done five mile he waves and cries goodbye. I never hustled my cob, for I found I could go by when I liked. Two mile from Dorking I gives the cob his head. Lord love you, he can do seventeen inside the hour, and he left that juggins as if he was standing still. When he drove up at Dorking, he says, 'You're a red-hot member!' and, by God, I think I am!"

This interesting yarn was received with rapture, and a remarkably strong anecdote of a lady and her footman fell flat, much to Mr. Preston's disgust. Then came the hour for personalities. As the drink takes effect our parlour customers attempt satire, and their efforts are always of a strongly personal nature.

"If I'd a boiled beetroot face like you, I'd never show my 'ed in a public room again."

"What's your wrong end like, you bloomin' Dutchman?"

"You shouldn't kiss and tell." (Rapturous applause.)

"Get away. You're too mean and miserable to do anything but count your dibs. He's so mean, gentlemen, that when he dropped a sixpence into the plate at church instead of a fourpenny-piece, he stopped his wife's cat's-meat allowance for a week to make up."

"If I had a voice like you I'd have it stuffed."

"If I had a nose like you I'd pay no more gas bills. You know your wife emptied the water-jug on you that night when you were lying boozed, because she thought it was a red-hot cinder on the floor."

And so on. The company part without any goodwill, and a night of odious stupidity is over. Personally, I regard every hour I have spent in this public-house as wasted. I never in my life heard a word of real fun, or real sense, excepting from men who were merely casual visitors. The person whose mind is satisfied by the parlour dullness of that nightly foolery only becomes animated when he is indecent. In tracing the natural history of a public-house I have found the respectable dullards the most revolting of my subjects.

But the mere fact that our one wretched hole is stupid and sometimes revolting by no means proves that all other places are of the same sort. I know one quiet, cleanly room where many smart young fellows go; their trade compels them to be decorous, and you see nothing but courtesy, and hear much good-natured and sensible chat.

The riverside 'Arry is always an awful being, but the gentle, respectful lad who takes his lemonade and enjoys himself in German fashion is nice company. I have seen all sorts, and, while I would gladly burst a 13-inch shell in such a cankered doghole as The Chequers, I am bound to say that there are a few cosy, harmless places whereof the loss would be a calamity.

* * * * *

I grow weary now, and often at nights, when the vast shadow of the lamp shudders on the ceiling and the wind moans hoarsely outside, I fall back in sheer luxury on the fine, straight, cut-and-thrust of old Boswell's conversations as a relief from the slavering babble which I often hear. Being a Loafer is all very good so far; but some of the men (and women) who address me use a kind of familiarity that makes me long to lie down and die. A man never loses the dandy instinct, and when you come to be actually addressed in familiar, or even impudent, terms by a sort of promoted housemaid, it makes you long for the soft-voiced, quiet ladies to whom a false accent or a shrill word would be a horror.

So long as you are a Loafer you must be prepared to put up with much. The better-class artisan is always a gentleman who never offers nor endures a liberty; but some of the flash sort are unendurable, and their womenkind are worse. With costers and bargemen one can always get on familiarly: it is the pretentious, vulgar men and females who are horrible.

Often and often I am tempted to creep back among the lights again, and feel the old delicate joy from cultured talk, lovely music, steady refinement, and beauty. Then comes the reckless fit, and I am off to The Chequers. Here is a rhyme which takes my fancy. I suppose it is my own, but have quite forgotten:—

This is the skull of a man,
    Soon shall your head be as empty:
Laugh and be glad while you can.

* * * * *

Where, from the silver that rims it,
    Glows the red spirit of wine,
Once there was longing and passion,
    Finding a woman divine;
    Blurred is the finished design,

This was the scope of the plan:
    Death, the dry Jester's old bauble—
Drink and be glad while you can.

Sorry and cynical symbol,
    Ghastly old caricature,
We, too, must walk in thy footsteps,
    We but a little endure.
    Bah! since the end is so sure,
Let us out-frolic our span,
    Death is a hush and a darkness—
Drink and be glad while you can.

A QUEER CHRISTMAS.

The Loafer seems to have fancied the company of seamen a great deal. At The Chequers few of the saltwater fellows fore-gathered, but when they did our Loafer was never long in picking them up. Here is one of the yarns which he heard. It is stuck in the Diary without reference to date, place of hearing, or anything else.

Joe Glenn used to say that the queerest Christmas Day he ever spent fell in 1883, the year of the great gale. In that year there was cruel trouble, and the number of folks wearing mourning that one met in Hull and Yarmouth, and the other places, was enough to make the most light-hearted man feel miserable. Black everywhere—nothing but black at every turn; and then the women's faces looked so wistful, and the children seemed so quiet, that I couldn't bear to walk the streets. The women would question any stranger that came from the quays, and they scorned to think that there was not always a chance for their men; but the dead seamen were swinging about in the ooze far down under the grey waves, and the poor souls who went gaping and gazing day after day had all their trouble for nothing.

Glenn towed out on the 20th of October, and he cried, "Goodbye, Sal; back for Christmas!" as they surged away toward Gorleston. Joe was mate of the Esperanza, and he was a very promising chap. He knew his way about the North Sea blindfold, and all he didn't know about his trade wasn't worth knowing. If you had asked him who Mr. Gladstone was he would probably have said, "I've heerd on him," but he could not have told you anything about Mr. Gladstone or any other statesman. So far as the world ashore went, Joe was as ignorant as a five-year-old child, and you would have laughed till you cried had you seen his delight when the pictures in a nursery-book were explained to him. It is hardly possible to imagine the existence of a grown man who is ignorant of things that are known to a child in the infant school; but there are many such knocking about at sea. What can you expect? They live amid the moaning desolation of that sad sea all the year round; they never used to have any schooling, and their world even now is limited by the blank horizon, with the rail of their boat for inner barrier. Glenn could very nearly read Moore's Almanac, and, as that great work was the only literature on board, he often interpreted it, and he was counted a great scholar. Then, he could actually use a sextant, and his way of working out his latitude was chaste and picturesque. Supposing he made the sun 29 deg. 18 min., and the declination for the day was 6 deg. 34 min. 22 sec., then he put down his figures this way:—

$$8948$$
$$2918$$
$$6300$$
$$634$$
$$5356$$

and when his chums saw him working out this profound calculation on the side of a bucket or on the companion hatch, they would say, "He's a wonnerful masterpiece. Yea, but he is, and nothin' but that."

Glenn was daring—but that is nothing to say, for all the fishermen seem insensible to fear. He was only once scared, and that was when he found a man leaning against the boat one pitch-dark night, just after the fishers had hauled. Joe thought the fellow was loafing, so he hit him a clout on the head, and made very uncomplimentary remarks. The victim of the assault took it very coolly, and one of the crew shouted—

"Don't touch that theer! He come up in the net while you was below."

118

Then Joe looked at the face, and when he found he had been punching a dead man he was sick.

But under any ordinary circumstances you couldn't shake the man's nerve, and he was fit to go anywhere, and do anything so far as the sea was concerned.

The Esperanza got up to her consorts, and then the usual toilsome monotony of the fisherman's life began. At the end of a month Joe looked a pretty object, for he had not washed himself all the time, and his hair and beard were like rough felt matting. There isn't much time for washing in the winter, and the fellows often go for a couple of months without feeling any water, except from the seas that are shipped. After the month was over the men began to pick up heart, and they notched off the days on the beams with much enjoyment.

Joe was like most of the fishermen: he liked to talk to the gulls. You see, when you are knocking around for a couple of months, you soon tire of your own shipmates, and there is no one else to talk with. The sea mostly makes it awkward to put out a boat except for purely business purposes, and you gradually get into the way of taking delight in small things. Joe would go aft, and call, "Kittee, Kittee—come, Kittee!" Then with superb curves the lovely gulls swept round, and remained delicately poised over the stern. Joe flung pieces of fish into the air, and kept chatting volubly as his pets swooped and squabbled. "Go and tell them we're coming, Kittee, my prittee. Only twenty days more and round she goes. Tell them we're all well, you sluts, and you'll have plenty of fish when we run out again." The gulls are the fisherman's friends, and the men insist on crediting the beautiful, rapacious birds with an accurate knowledge of human affairs.

So the days flew by, and the time came when sugar—the seaman's luxury in winter—began to run short. That was enough to make the fellows sick for home, and they were ready to dance for joy when the gay flag was hoisted at last. Gaily the Esperanza rattled through the fleet, and envious men cried "What cheer!" in a doleful manner. After a twelve hours' run the wind fell away, and the sky began to look funny. Hoarse

119

vague noises came over the sea, and it seemed as if certain sounds were growing weary and swooning away. Little breaths of air came softly—oh, so softly, and so deadly cold!—but the tiny puffs were hardly enough to send a feather far. The birds wailed a good deal, and when the ducks began to cry "Karm, kah-ah-arm," the men shouted, "Billee, run, Billee; or I'll bring the policeman!" for all the chaps hate to hear the ducks yawping.

Clouds of haze moved around, and when the moon came up she seemed to be glowering from her shroud. Joe was anxious to take in something, but the skipper said, "Don't think there'll be much of it. We can reef her when it comes away. I want to be home." All the night it seemed as though something evil were in the air, and even the men below were depressed. Sometimes it happens that if you work long in a lonely house, you find yourself at night living in dread of some vague ill, and every crack of the woodwork is like an ominous message. It is just that way at sea before a bad gale.

When Joe saw the moon beginning to paint the clouds with leprous hues, and the great ring grew wider and wider, he looked at the mainsail, and wished the trouble over. At midnight there came a sigh; then a rattle of blocks, and then a big, silent wave came pouring along. Something was astir somewhere, and before long the Esperanza's crew knew what was the matter. The last glare of wild-fire flushed the sky, and then down came the breeze. The Esperanza was as stiff as a house, but it made her lie over a little, and she roared along in fine style. In two hours the vessel was putting her lee rail nearly under, and a single sharp squall would have hove her down, so the hands were called up to reef her. Joe was out on the boom, getting the reef-earrings adrift, when the first of the chapter of accidents came. A man sang out, "Look out for a drop o' water!" and a black mountain smashed over the Esperanza in an instant after. Joe saw the third hand slip, and the next second the man was whisked overboard. The Esperanza was still smothered, and a stab of pity went through Joe's heart as he saw his shipmate wallowing. But he had no time for sentiment;

he grabbed the reef-earring with his left hand, and clutched at the man with his right. When the vessel shook herself, both good fellows came inboard, and hung on panting. "No time to lose," said Joe; and indeed there wasn't. The spoondrift began to fly so that you could not see the moon, and the wind was enough to choke you if you faced it. I have heard Joe say that small shot couldn't have hit you very much harder than the drift when you looked to windward. Then the sea was growing worse every minute, until at last every man on board except the skipper wanted to let her ride. But the worthy captain said, "If she's got to be smothered, she'll be smothered moving. The nearer to home the nearer to help, and she shall go." So the Esperanza tore on throughout the awful night with all four of her reefs in, and it was a mercy, that she was never badly hit. At dawn the rushing hills of water were travelling like lightning. It was just as though some mighty power had set an Alpine district moving, and when a vessel soared over the crown of a grey mountain she looked like a mere seabird. In the valleys of this mad, winding mountain range the whistling hurricane raved and whirled, and the drift that was plucked looked like smoke from some hellish cauldron. And still the grizzled old skipper would go on, though it was touch-and-go every time a sequence of strong seas came howling down. The foresail went, and that was bad; but those fine seamen do not ever come to the end of their resources so long as life lasts, and they got ready to set another as soon as the wind showed the least sign of fining off. The Esperanza tore onward, lunging violently, and shaking as though she dreaded the grip of some savage pursuer. No wonder the seamen speak of a vessel as if she had intelligence; there is something so strangely vivid in the expression of a ship that it cannot be expressed in words, and I shall not try.

At length Joe sang out, "I reckon that's the Galloper, skipper."

"Right you are, chap! And what's that by the edge of the broken water? Wessel, I fancy."

"'Tis a barque, skipper, and he's got 'em flyin'."

The two men watched the vessel a long time, and they determined to run down on her as near as might be safe. As they drew on her it appeared that she was not actually hard-and-fast, but she was bumping apparently, and they guessed she had her anchors out. There is nothing in the way of close shaves that a smacksman will not venture, and the Esperanza was soon within speaking distance.

"We have a pilot aboard!" sang out someone on deck.

"A lightning sort of pilot to ram her nose on the Galloper!" growled the old skipper. "Do you want any assistance?"

"Stand by for a bit and we'll see."

So the Esperanza went to leeward of the shoal and hove-to. Presently the stranger signalled, "Come on board of us."

Then Joe said, "That fellow's in a frap before his time, skipper. I believe she'll come off when the tide turns. If she does, and we have her in charge, that's a nice lump of money for all of us."

"But how are we going to get to him?"

"I'll go," said Joe. "Give me old Bill, and we'll take the boat down on him. You get the trawl warp ready, and we'll either tow him or steer him."

"Right, chap; over with your boat, lads!"

Then Bill lay down in the boat, Joe put an oar in the sculling-notch, and the little thing flew before wind and sea, while the smack drew off a little. Presently the bulge of the boat's bow glanced along the ship's side, and Joe flung his painter. Then a man clambered on to the rail, and Joe roared, "Where are you coming to?"

"I'm the pilot, and I'm coming aboard of you."

"That you're not, you blasted coward! Stay where you are, and we'll see if we can't save the wessel."

But the pilot had lost his head. He got ready for a jump; the boat lifted, and he sprang; the backwash pushed her out, and the man's left foot only just touched the gunwale. He screamed like a woman, gripped vainly at the air, and rolled under. A sea drove his head against the ship's side; the boat swung with tremendous force. Scraunch! and the poor fellow was gone, with his head crushed like a walnut. Joe tried to grab him with the boathook, but it was useless, and the unhappy poltroon's body was whirled away.

"Here's a nice go for a start! Up with you, Billy!"

Then the two fishermen gained the deck, and found not a soul to meet them. "Where the devil are they all?" Joe ran forward, and went below. In the dim light he could see little, but he heard a sound as of men moaning, and as his sight became accustomed to the dusk he saw several swarthy fellows kneeling. They were kissing their crucifixes and making a woeful noise. Joe yelled, "Where's your skipper?" but no one heeded him, and the moaning prayers went on. With a curse Joe rushed aft. On his way he saw the sounding rod, and he shouted, "See how much she's got in her, Bill. There's a set of mounseers forrad there, no more good than kittens."

Then the mate entered the after-cabin, and found a man on the floor. "What cheer, O, what cheer! Tumble up, my daisy!"

The man glared glassily, and muttered, "I speak him Ingleese very good."

"Never mind your Ingleese; come on, and make your fellows help to pump." The captain rose, reeled, and fell. He was mortal drunk.

"You been do you dam please," he hiccupped; and Joe retired with a shrug.

It was clear that the English pilot had run a Spanish ship aground, as nearly as possible, and only the two anchors kept her from going hard on. The two Englishmen found that the vessel had five feet of water in her, and, in their plain, matter-of-fact way, they set to work. Ugly washes were coming over, but they lashed themselves to the pump and set to work like the indomitable seadogs that they were. They could not make her suck, but before they were utterly exhausted they reduced the water much, and then they cast themselves clear and began to prepare for the tide. They put the fore topsail on her, and then signalled for their own vessel. With a last effort they got one anchor, but, when Joe proposed trying the other, poor Billy groaned, "That's a pill enough for me, Joe; I shall die if we stand to it any more. Slip the other cable, boy." Joe agreed; the anchor was lost, and the men prepared for the first creak that would show that the tide was coming. The sea seemed to be fining off a bit, so they looked round, and found to their horror that the rudder was gone. She wallowed. "There she goes, Bill. But Lord, what a job! Tell you, the smack must go under bare poles; we'll make her fast aft, and she'll steer us."

This was a genuine seamanlike idea, for, of course, the drag of the smack would steady the barque, and the two vessels could crawl along with some approach to surety. Another roll and groaning of timbers, then came a lull and a flaw of wind; the topsail pulled, and, with a long grind, the barque rolled off into deep water.

"Hooray! Let her drift as she likes till the skipper gets to us."

Bill jumped into the boat and guided her down wind to the Esperanza. The smack came close round, another hand joined Bill, and in half an hour a couple of warps were made fast to the Spaniard, and the two vessels went on in procession. They could not do so much as a knot per hour, but, at all events, they were drawing into open water, and the smack steered the barque quite true.

It was a pity that a second hand did not remain with Joe, but no one foresaw what would happen. The good mate went below forward, and found the men worse than ever from drink, panic, and religion. He tried all he knew to fetch them on deck, but nothing would serve. He tried the captain, but that worthy seaman was sleeping like a hog, and the cognac was running in slavers from his mouth.

"Shouldn't wonder if he has 'em on when he starts on the beer again," muttered Joe. He saw a large sheath-knife, and secured that in his own belt; then he took a mouthful of wine, and went to his post.

There was plenty of sea, but the prize was far too valuable to be left, and Glenn determined to make a bold bid for fortune. Not a single vessel passed them all night, and they were lonely at dawn next day. The sailors crept up one by one, but they only gathered in a jabbering knot, and scowled at the Englishman heavily. Joe made signs for them to turn-to at the pumps, but they scowled still more. Then he signed that he wanted something to eat, but the fellows only looked venomous, and poor Joe groaned, "Tomorrow's Christmas Day, and no tommy to eat—let be the pudden!"

It was indeed heartrending; but the skipper was a thoughtful man, and when he found that his mate was famine-struck, he risked swamping the boat, and sent some beef and biscuit. The shameless Spaniards had plenty below, but they were enraged for some reason or other, and they would have let their deliverer hunger himself to the bone.

That evening, while Joe was easing the warps by shoving pieces of coir where the bite came, he felt a grip on his neck. Like a flash he thought, "Now, the knife." He wrenched himself round, and there was the Spanish captain, glaring, trembling, and breathing hard.

"See, see! You been help, Ingleese!" and he pointed to the dusk as he shrieked.

Joe saw at once that the man was wild with drink, and he put on a smile, with a notion of coaxing the captain over. In a little while he managed to get him below, and, foolishly, filled him some more cognac. Joe thought it best to stupefy the fellow, and the brandy certainly did send him to sleep.

That was a bad night, for the wind rose again, and such a sea ran that Glenn gave up hope at midnight, and got ready for the worst. At the dawn of Christmas Day the skipper offered to relieve him, but the risk would have been too much, and the dogged East Coaster stuck to his work, though he was aching, drenched, and so sleepy that he did not know how to keep his eyes open.

A queer Christmas? Yes, but not much more queer than the Christmas passed by thousands of good fellows on that treacherous great channel. The warps both parted with an awful jerk at noon, just as Joe was about to drink a dismal health to Sal with some of the captain's cognac. He took a look round, and, though I cannot say that his courage went, I am bound to tell you that a kind of ferocious despair seized on him when he found the barque yawing away from the Esperanza. She might broach-to any time, and then all would be over. Poor Joe! Not a soul was there to comfort him. The Spanish sluggards came up sometimes and scowled, then they went below again. It was cruel work. The skipper of the Esperanza made desperate efforts to get up, but dusk fell before he came near, and then it was too late to try anything especially as the barque was going yard-arm under. Dark fell, and Joe heard moaning and gibbering once more. The captain was creeping along the deck, "saying something about Madd-ray," as Joe put it. "It was him as was mad," the smacksman said, with an attempt at humour. "He made a try to stick me, and I felt something sting my arm like a pin going in."

That was true. The maddened drunkard made a staggering attempt to stab Glenn, and then, with a yell, he poised on the rail and jumped into the sea.

That was really about enough for one Christmas Day, and Joe's nerve was all gone.

The cold seemed to grip his blood, for he had taken little good nourishment; the vessel was helpless, and there was no shelter from the flying rivers of water that came over. Joe felt that strange, hard pain across the brows that seizes a man who has been long sleepless, and he could have dozed off had it not been for the continual breaking of the seas. He saw the Esperanza's lights, and he wished that the boat could have been sent, if it were only to give him a little company. The rolling of the barque was awful at two in the morning, and, at last, one violent kick parted the mizen rigging on the starboard side. Then came one vast roll, and a ponderous rush of water, and with a tearing crash, the mast went over the side.

Joe edged his way forward, and once more spoke to the gang in the forecastle. By dint of signs he made them understand that he wanted a hatchet, and he also contrived to let them know that they must go down unless the port rigging was severed. For a wonder he got what he wanted, and he laboured until his elbows were numbed before the bumping, rolling mast was clear.

Four hours till daylight, and wind and sea getting worse. Something must be done, or the strained ship would go for a certainty; it only wanted one unlucky sea to settle her. But what could one man do? If two of the sodden ruffians forrad would only come up, then something might be done; but one tired sailor was of little use. Glenn resolved to make one more appeal to the Spaniards, for he had a bright plan in his head, and he needed no more than the aid of two men to carry it out. A spare mainyard was lashed out on deck, and Joe had noticed it with the seaman's quick eye when he came on board. If he could only get hold of a spare topsail he could save the vessel, and he was ready to go on his knees to the men if they would show him a sail locker. After imploring, cursing threatening, for five minutes, Joe at last got the mate to lug out a sail; then he persuaded a lad who was more sober than the rest to come on deck with a lantern. Now, it will be noticed that foreign seamen in general are dreadfully afraid of taking to the boat. During this present winter our fellows have saved four or five foreign crews, and in every case the vessels had their own boats undamaged, but the men dursn't risk the trip themselves, so our fishermen had to peril their lives. The Spaniard's boat was lashed so that no mortal could get her clear, and the little craft was used as a sort of lumber-closet. Glenn had noticed some steel rails in the boat, and he guessed that these specimens of railway plant were accidentally left out until the hatches had been battened down.

He thanked God for the negligence.

Working with desperate speed, he rudely bent the spare sail to the spar; then to the lower cloth of the sail he managed to fix two of the weighty rails, and then commenced to lug the yard past the vessel's foremast. It takes a long time to tell all this, but Joe was not long, though every movement was made at the risk of his life. He hacked away two lengths of rope measuring each about eighty feet; he made these into bridles, knotting one end of each piece to the end of the spar, and taking the other ends round the timber-heads. Two pieces of thin rope, hauled out of the hamper aft, were made fast to the ends of the steel rails, and then Joe made a frantic effort to get his apparatus over the side. No good; he must humiliate himself again before those unspeakable aliens. Drenched, agonised for lack of sleep, weak with exertion, and bleeding from the hustling blows that he had received, the poor soul besought the men to lend him a hand, and swore to save them. They understood him fast enough, and one peculiarly drunken individual blundered up and obeyed Glenn's signs. With a violent effort the spar was hoisted and dropped; the steel rails sank, and there was an apparatus like an enormous window-blind hanging in the water. The barque soon felt the pull of this novel anchor; she swung round, with her head to the sea, and to Joe's passionate delight she rode more softly, for the big spar broke every sea, and very little water came on board afterwards. The vessel was securely moored, for she could not drag that great expanse of canvas through the seas.

When the grey light rose, there was quite plenty of sea, but the barque was all right, and so was Joe, for he had coolly gone below, and he fell asleep, with a thankful heart, on the cabin bench. The ship was quiet as a cradle, and the smack's boat got up to her easily. The warps were made fast again, and the two vessels once more went away in procession.

This time Joe had English company, and the two men had a good time until the tug picked them up off Lowestoft. Joe Glenn had not changed a stitch for eleven days, but he did not mind the discomfort the lump of salvage made up for much pain and striving.

Joe bought a good cottage with his share, and he was satisfied; but I quite agreed with him when he said that his money was hard earned. No man ever spent a much queerer Christmas.

JACK BROWN.

When I first saw Jack, he had left his vessel at Barking Creek, and he was enjoying a very vigorous spree; but he never lost temper or became stupefied, and his loud merriment was rather pleasant than otherwise. Jack did not look by any means like a rough, for his face had a kind of girlish beauty. His dark cheeks were richly flushed, his throat was round and white, and his blue eyes twinkled with fun. He stood about six feet in height, and he would have made a fine guardsman, for he looked as if he had been carefully drilled all his life long. Men who habitually exercise every muscle and tendon acquire that graceful carriage which belongs to the military gymnast. This fine young fellow was full of high spirits and bodily power; courage was so natural to him that I do not think such a word as "brave" ever entered his vocabulary. He had never been afraid of anything in his life, and it did not occur to him to think of danger. When Jack was a little child he was taken out to sea in his father's vessel, and henceforth a ship was his only home from year's end to year's end. The boy was so daring that he made some of the old hands nervous very often, and there were many doleful prophecies made regarding the ultimate fate of his carcase. On one blowy day when the ships were pitching freely, it happened that Jack's father went with fish to the steam cutter, leaving the urchin on deck. As the old man drew back within a quarter-mile of his smack, he saw a black figure clambering along the gaff, and he knew that it was Jack. Young Hopeful crawled from the throat of the gaff to the very end of the spar, and then proceeded to swarm up the gaff halyards—a most perilous proceeding. The father was aghast; he whispered hurriedly, "Pull, for God's sake; she'll roll him overboard before we get up." But the young monkey did not part with his hold so easily, and he came down by the rings of the mainsail without so much as grazing his shins.

In every vessel the men must have a plaything, and Jack served his bigger comrades admirably in that capacity. Had not his father been on board, the lad might have been ill-used in the horrible way so common in the old days; but the stern skipper allowed no rough play, and the boy was merely set on to perform harmless tricks. Once the men dared him to climb down the bobstay, and he instantly tried; but he gave the crew a scare, for he could not climb back after the vessel had dipped him a few times, and, last of all, the boat was towered to rescue him. In hard weather and amid hard work, Jack grew steadily in strength and skill. I have seen him at work and he made me shudder, although the sight of his amazing agility might have given anybody confidence. On wet nights when the deck was like a rink, he would make a rush as the boat pitched; then he would pick up his rope unerringly in the dark and, in another second, you would see him over the side with one foot on the trawl-beam in an attitude risky enough to make you want to close your eyes.

It was nothing much to see him take a flying spring on to the main boom in the dark, and hang there reefing while the vessel jerked so that you might have fancied she must send his ribs through the skin. I say it was nothing, because he performed this feat nearly every winter night, after the midnight haul, and the spectacle grew common. I never knew him bungle over a rope or make a bad slip, and it was simply a pleasure to see him steer. He never threw away an inch, and his way of stealing foot by foot was worthy of any jockey. Sometimes when I was at the wheel and running a little to leeward of another vessel, he would say, "I reckon I can weather him, sir, if you let me have her a bit;" and then, with delicate touches and catlike watching of every puff and every send of the sea, he would edge his way up, and pass his opponent neatly.

Most wonderful of all it was to see Jack handling the small boat in heavy weather. While the wee cockle-shell was rolling and bungling under our quarter, he would jump on the rail, measure his distance perfectly, spring on to the boat's gunwale and fend her off before she made the return roll. A marvellous performance that was, and the marvel only increased when you saw the young fellow pitching heavy boxes of fish on to the deck of the great steam cutter.

With a roar, and a savage sweep the big seas came; on their mountainous sides the shrill eddies of wind played, and the lines of foam twined in wavering mazes. Hill on hill gathered, and the seas looked like swelling Downs piled heap on heap, while the sonorous crests roared on hoarsely, and sometimes the face of the wild water was obscured in the white smoke plucked off by the gusts.

Jack did not mind weather; the steamer hurled herself up on the bulge of a sea, and then you could get a glimpse of a tall, lithe figure, straining in the small boat alongside the rearing iron hulk. That splendid, lithe young lad performed prodigies of strength and courage; the hulk and the little boat sank down,—down until the steamer's mast-head disappeared; then with a rush the wave slid away, and the craft came toppling down the hither side of the mountain, and still that lithe figure was there, toiling fiercely and cleverly. Soon with a bound and a loud laugh, he was on board of us again, and no one could tell from one tremor of his merry, tawny face that he had been, of a truth, looking into the very jaws of death.

This splendid man was innocent as a child of all worldly affairs unconnected with the sea. He once told me, "I can make a shift to get along with an easy book; but if I come to a hard word, I cry 'Wheelbarrows,' and skip him." On his own topics he was very sensible, and no owner could have found fault with him had he not been just a little racketty on shore. In my refined days I remember reading in one of Thackeray's books about a young lord who was much loved by one Henry Esmond: My friend Jack was very like that young man, and you could not get vexed with him,—or, at any rate, you could not keep vexed very long.

We soon made friends in The Chequers, and before midnight we were confidential. On my expressing wonder at seeing a Barking lad among us,

131

Jack winked with profound meaning, and said, "I ain't Barking at all, only for this trip. My gal's a Lowestoft gal, and she've come up here, so I'm ready for her Sunday out tomorrow. See?"

Our second interview took place next day, and I saw the sweetheart. She was an ordinary pretty servant-girl, such as most of the fishermen pick up when they marry out of their own class; but I could see that she was likely to make some difference in John's rather convivial habits. She spoke like an ignorant woman with strong natural sense, and when Jack proposed having some beer, she said, "Ay, so! That's the way you fare to go. I've seen them, as soon as ever they leaves the pay-office, turning into the public-house. And a master lot o' good that do, doan't it now? Men workin' like beasts for two months, and then dropping all their money into the till in a week, and then off to sea short of clothes, besides very likely getting into trouble. Nay! Have yow a glass of ale if yow care, but no good never come on it, what I know. Leastways, not for men that goes to the sea."

So Jack and I deferred to Sally's opinion—until nine o'clock in the evening, and then we made up for lost time. It was amusing to see the cool way in which the handsome lad parted from his sweetheart. They had not met for two months, and yet I do not believe that they exchanged kisses either at meeting or parting.

These folk are strangely undemonstrative. They are fond of each other, and most faithful, but they show nothing. On a grim morning after a gale, when the vessels are towing up with flags half-mast high, the women will gather on the tow-path and by the quays; you see white, drawn faces, but rarely a tear. The bleak, perilous life of the men seems to be known intimately to the women, and they accept the worst fortune with a dry pathos that is heartbreaking. Jack and his sweetheart were in the flush of youth—nay, of physical beauty; they were passionately fond of each other; and they parted like casual strangers. When Jack went again below to the filthy, frowsy cabin of the smack, and thought over the months of cold, toil, drenching weather, and hard fare, I have no doubt but that he thought of the pretty girl, but he said very little, and larked on as usual as soon as he got over his parting carouse.

For several trips after this, my handsome fellow was wild and careless; his splendid constitution enabled him to drink with impunity the abominable stuff sold by the Copers, and he was merely merry when older soakers were delirious. His father and he parted, and the old man stayed at home as ship's husband to a firm of smack owners, and the lad had his head free. He was as desperately brave as ever, for the subtle poison was long in attacking his nerve; but many of his ways were queer, and the men who went home in the returning smacks carried unpleasant reports about him. At times, like Robert Burns, George Morland, and men of that kidney, he would give way to a passionate burst of repentance; but in his case the repentance always departed with the return of health and buoyancy.

One night he stayed on board a coper until a breeze came away; he then insisted on straddling across the bow of the boat on the return journey, and he lost his grip for once in his life and went overboard. A dip of that sort, with heavy sea-boots on, is rather dangerous, and Master Jack felt as though all the water in the North Sea was dragging at his legs; but he was hauled in at last. Even that experience only cured him for a week, and then his resorts to the brandy-bottle began again.

At last, when he was putting fish aboard the carrier, a letter was handed to him; he looked at it with rough tenderness, and crammed it, all greasy and gruesome, under his jumper. On getting aboard, he went to a quiet corner where the men could not tease, and he read,

"Dear John,—I write these few lines hoping you are quite well as this leaves me at present, but i don't think as you can be well if all is trew as we hear you are very wild and you ont have no money to come home if you doant watshe it. You must either stop the beer or stop goin with me and then my heart would be broak, every girl I see which married a drinking man has supped sorrow for sertain, and the man the same, and you will be just the same. Pray, my dear, do take the right tirning, or I

133

must keap my word. So no more at present from your loveing SARAH KERRISON."

Jack cursed once, and then muttered "Werra well, let her. Let her go and take on some one better;" but he was amazingly unhappy despite his defiance, and his unhappiness drove him to frantic excesses. He used to scare his companions by saying, "If God takes my girl, they can talk about Him as they like, but He shan't take my soul, not if I damn for it." Then when the shuddering men said, "For mercy's sake, shut up. It's enough to sink the wessel," he would make answer, "Werra good, let her sink; and the sooner the better."

The days wore away, and the time came for Jack to run home. The smack was well clear of the fleets and spinning along nicely to southward on a dark night, and Jack was at the wheel. His nerve was just a little touched, and he muttered, "This is a devil of a night. I wish we were well home."

It was indeed a weird night; the wind thrummed on the cordage; the gaff whistled with tremulous sounds, as though some frightened soul were shivering at the mast-head; and when the inky waves rolled out of the gloom, they showed no definite shape—only a sliding dark cloud fringed with white flame. There is always a steady roar from the sails, and one hears it better at night; Jack had often heard the roar rise to a howl, but no noise that ever he knew had such effect on him as the rushing moan from the sails that night.

There are only two men in a watch on board a smack, and it often happens that one will go below to fetch some of the tea which the seamen drink so insatiably. Jack's mate was below, but the helmsman had no fear, as all was clear. He mused on, always peering sharply round for a few minutes when suddenly, over the haze which was rising, he saw a white light, and then the loom of a green. "All right; well clear," he muttered. "Glad the fog's no higher. Why doesn't he use his whistle?" Then, with the suddenness of lightning, he found the red light opened on him, and, with a chill at his heart, he discovered that he could not get his own vessel out of the road. Once he sang out, and then came the looming of a black mountain over him. Until the monster's stem took him on the quarter and the smack hurled over—hustled into the sea by the impetus of the steamer—Jack never left go of his wheel; he had a few seconds, and, with his nimble spring, he rushed to the mizen rigging, nicked the strings of one lifebuoy; lifted another from forward of the companion, and then made his rush for the forehatch.

"All out. No time for the boats!"

One man sprang up panting and Jack said, "Here you are, Harry. Shove that on, and jump. Jump to windward." The smack reared up; there was a long crashing rush of the swift water; then Jack saw the liquid darkness over him, and he was just beginning to hear that awful buzzing in the ears when, with a roar, he felt the upper air swoop round him.

He could just see a coil of foam on the blackness to mark where the smack had gone down, and, as he cleared his eyes, he saw the cloudy shape of the steamer far away. "Harry, boy!" he sang out, but Harry must have been hit by a spar, and Jack Brown was left alone on that bleak, black waste of wandering water.

"A lingering death," he murmured, as he felt the spray cut round his head; but he struggled resolutely to keep his face front the set of the sea, and the buoy supported him bravely. His thoughts ran on things past; he had spoken unkindly of Sally, behind her back; he had been tipsy—Ah! how often! Then he thought, "Shall I pray and repent?" All the daredevil in the deluded lad's soul arose at this question, and he snarled "No. Blowed if I snivel just yet, only because I'm in a bad way." Oh, Jack, Jack! And the deep grave weltering below you, and only a ring of cork and oilskin to keep you out of that cold home. Was there never a shudder as you thought of the crowding fishes? Their merciless cold eyes! Their grey, slimy skin! But Jack was at that day a reckless fellow, and he lived to be passionately sorry for his splenetic madness.

The cold grew worse and worse, and it seemed to creep toward Jack's heart. He gave one cry, and instantly he heard a faint answer. Could it be the scream of a gull? Nay, they rest at night. He called again, and the voice of his agony was answered by a loud hail; then a flare was lit, and Jack knew that the steamer's boat had been searching for him.

"Easy. Shove the painter under his arms, and then two of you haul."

So Jack was plumped into the boat, and lay limp and sick. In an hour he was warm asleep in his berth on board the steamer, and, I am afraid to say that he begged hard for a pipe before he dozed over.

The steamer took him home, and he was received in a matter-of-fact way by his people. He had had a dousing! Yes, but it was all in the day's work. That is the way in which the good folk talk.

Jack was never the same again, and some of the old men said "he looked as if he had seen something." Yes, he had seen something, and he said to Sally, "All right about that letter of yours. Let it stick to the wall." The man was very grave and kind, and he spoke freely to those of his cronies who were on shore; but he would not go near his old haunts, and some people thought he must have got religious. Perhaps he had. At any rate something that happened not long afterwards made the supposition probable. Jack was on the Ter Schelling bank when his turn came to go home again, and he was moodily wondering whether any such ordeal would ever be put on him as that which he endured when the steamer sank his vessel.

The weather looked ugly; the glass went fast down, and a wild and leprous-looking moon shone lividly through a shifting mask of troubled clouds. A sullen calm fell, and the smack rolled with clashing blocks and groaning spars, making night hideous. In the morning a gale broke and soon came a blinding fall of snow. It was impossible to see many yards through the rushing drift of murky yellow, but Jack took in all four reefs, and ran on with a rag of sail and a three-cloth jib.

It was not a sea that came away; it was a mere enormous cataract that poured on irresistibly. Jack knew that so long as he could keep the boat moving, he might escape having his decks stove in, so he determined to try it—neck or nothing. No man on board knew when the sea might come which would heave her down, and they watched grimly as the gallant craft tore on. Some wanted to heave-to, but the skipper knew that he would stand a good chance of being smothered that way, and he resolved to get as near home as possible, in case the hurricane grew worse. After boring for ten hours in the worst of the tremendous sea, he saw a vessel to leeward of him, flying signals of distress. She was sinking, and her boat was smashed. The mate said, "That poor chap on't see land." Jack thought a little, and then he said, "I'm going to try. Out with your boat." Discipline on board the smacks is not very strict, and the men were inclined to question the wisdom of Jack's proposal; but Englishmen always lean to humanity, and with a little persuasion, all hands volunteered. Jack took one unmarried man, and then coolly proceeded to make his wild attempt. It was a forlorn kind of chance for everybody, but as Jack said, "I was saved once, and I know what them poor bloods feel like."

The little boat had first of all to run down on the sinking smack, and then, at the risk of capsizing, Jack's vessel ran to leeward and came round, sending everything shaking as she came up. Only desperately brave and supremely kindly people would have dared such a thing, and even the skipper of the foundering vessel said, "Well, chaps, I thought no one but a mad one would a-tried it on; but Gord bless you all the same."

After that, Jack was obliged to let go his anchor within sound of breakers, and his fight with death lasted all night. The lifeboats could not get out to him, and he could only pray that the snow-curtain might lift. In the morning a slant of wind came which enabled him to get away from the gnashing breakers, and he got in with the loss of his gaff. Sally was home for Christmas-time, and she was mighty proud when no less a person than the Mayor presented Jack with a town's subscription, which was quite enough to fit up a house.

Jack is my favourite of all the loose fish I have known, and if ever I take up my place again—alas!—I shall have him with me, and make him live ashore.

CPSIA information can be obtained
at www.ICGtesting.com
Printed in the USA
LVHW051804130623
749652LV00006B/298